ONLY LIGHT CAN DO THAT

60 DAYS OF MLK DEVOTIONS FOR KIDS

DR. MARTIN LUTHER KING JR.

WITH LISA A. CRAYTON AND SHARIFA STEVENS

ILLUSTRATED BY CAMILLA RU

PUBLISHED IN PARTNERSHIP WITH

An Imprint of Thomas Nelson

In Association with

License granted by Intellectual Properties Management, Inc., Atlanta GA, exclusive licensor of the King Estate.

Tommy Nelson titles may be purchased in bulk for educational, business, fundraising, or sales promotional use. For information, please e-mail SpecialMarkets@ThomasNelson.com.

Unless otherwise noted, Scripture quotations are taken from the International Children's Bible®. Copyright © 1986, 1988, 1999, 2015 by Thomas Nelson. Used by permission. All rights reserved.

Scripture quotations marked GNT are taken from the Good News Translation in Today's English Version—Second Edition. Copyright © 1992 by American Bible Society. Used by permission.

Scripture quotations marked NCV are taken from the New Century Version®. Copyright © 2005 by Thomas Nelson. Used by permission. All rights reserved.

Scripture quotations marked NIrV are taken from the Holy Bible, New International Reader's Version®, NIrV®. Copyright © 1995, 1996, 1998, 2014 by Biblica, Inc.® Used by permission of Zondervan. All rights reserved worldwide. www. Zondervan.com. The "NIrV" and "New International Reader's Version" are trademarks registered in the United States Patent and Trademark Office by Biblica, Inc.®

Scripture quotations marked NIV are taken from The Holy Bible, New International Version®, NIV®. Copyright © 1973, 1978, 1984, 2011 by Biblica, Inc.® Used by permission of Zondervan. All rights reserved worldwide. www.Zondervan. com. The "NIV" and "New International Version" are trademarks registered in the United States Patent and Trademark Office by Biblica, Inc.®

Scripture quotations marked NKJV are taken from the New King James Version®. Copyright © 1982 by Thomas Nelson. Used by permission. All rights reserved.

Scripture quotations marked NLT are taken from the Holy Bible, New Living Translation. © 1996, 2004, 2015 by Tyndale House Foundation. Used by permission of Tyndale House Ministries, Carol Stream, Illinois 60188. All rights reserved.

Scripture quotations marked TLB are taken from The Living Bible. Copyright © 1971. Used by permission of Tyndale House Publishers a division of Tyndale House Ministries, Carol Stream, Illinois 60188. All rights reserved.

ISBN 978-1-4002-4421-8 (audiobook)
ISBN 978-1-4002-4420-1 (eBook)
ISBN 978-1-4002-4419-5 (HC)

Library of Congress Cataloging-in-Publication Data on file

LCCN 2023027466

Written by Lisa A. Crayton and Sharifa Stevens

Illustrated by Camilla Ru

Printed in India

23 24 25 26 27   REP   10 9 8 7 6 5 4 3 2 1

Mfr: REP / Sonipat, India / November 2023 / PO #12179993

CONTENTS

PART 3: HOPE

PART 4: FORGIVENESS AND RECONCILIATION

PART 5: COMPASSION

PART 9: SACRIFICE

THE LIGHT OF DR. MARTIN LUTHER KING JR.

DR. MARTIN LUTHER KING JR.'S life was soaked in light.

As the son and grandson of pastors, young Martin learned early about God's light. Even before he could read the bright commands and promises in the Bible, he saw Jesus shine through the love of his parents, both for him and others. His father and mother taught him that hatred has no place in God's family. Martin treasured the words of his mother, Alberta: "You are as good as anyone," and the actions of his father, who fought against segregated elevators in the Atlanta courthouse.

The Lord's commands are pure. They light up the way.
PSALM 19:8

But young Martin's knowledge of God's light highlighted the sting of racism in his home state of Georgia. In his autobiography, he remembered a trip to the shoe store with his father. A store clerk said to Martin's dad:

"I'll be happy to wait on you if you'll just move to those seats in the rear."

Dad immediately retorted, "There's nothing wrong with these seats. We're quite comfortable here."

"Sorry," said the clerk, "but you'll have to move."

"We'll either buy shoes sitting here," my father retorted, "or we won't buy shoes at all."

Whereupon he took me by the hand and walked out of the store. . . . I still remember walking down the street beside him as he muttered, "I don't care how long I have to live with this system, I will never accept it."

As he grew up, Martin learned that following the light of Jesus didn't mean becoming blind to injustice but challenging it. Following Jesus meant fighting darkness. Young Martin studied knowledge and truth intensely. He skipped a grade in elementary school and completed high school by age fifteen. By age twenty-five, he had earned a doctoral degree in theology—the study of God.

Throughout his life, Martin Luther King Jr. made decisions to follow Jesus' light. This commitment led to his job as a pastor and his role as an *activist*, then to a position as the leader of a national civil rights movement.

Are you ready to learn more about Dr. King's work as an activist? First you have to understand that his actions were based in his Christian faith.

Christians believe that the way to walk in the light is to . . .

- believe that Jesus is the Son of God;
- believe that Jesus died as payment for the wrongs of all people in order to bring them back to God;
- believe that Jesus came back to life and now lives in heaven; and
- love God and love others.

The light of Jesus is no ordinary light. Jesus' light not only shines truth to make us aware of our wrongs; it shines forgiveness for those wrongs. Jesus' light shines to bring us close to God and close to each other. Jesus' goal was *reconciliation*. He didn't come to punish the world, but to bring the world back to a relationship with the God of light.

RECONCILIATION: bringing back together two people who are separated

Jesus shared His light generously. He offered rest, healing, and truth to all sorts of people: women, men, and children; thieves and traitors; leaders and poor people; Brown, Black, and White. Jesus never

used violence to defend Himself when people were angry with what He said. He did everything with peace and love, and He invited people to follow His example. He even remained peaceful when He was unfairly accused and condemned to die by leaders who saw His light as a threat. The leaders, both religious and governmental, liked things the way they were. They plotted to put out the light of Jesus by killing Him. But they failed. Jesus rose from the dead, and His light shines to this day.

Because he followed Jesus, Dr. King devoted himself to studying and preaching God's Word and caring for his community. In 1954, Dr. King began pastoring in Montgomery, Alabama. The next year, a Black woman named Rosa Parks refused to give up her bus seat in that same city, an event that changed Dr. King's life. In the southern United States, life was *segregated*. Black people were kept apart in schools, restaurants, churches, and stores. They could sit only in the back of a bus. When a White person wanted to sit in a crowded bus, a Black person had to give up her seat. Rosa's actions led to a *boycott,* which meant that Black protesters did not ride the buses until Black riders were treated with the same rights as White riders.

SEGREGATION: a system of separating people by race

BOYCOTT: a protest in which people act together to stop using or buying a product or service, or participating in an activity to oppose injustice

Dr. King's decision to lead the resulting bus boycott gave him another role: activist. From that time on, he committed completely to fighting the shadow of injustice, became the chief leader of the civil rights movement in the United States, and brought light to many of the country's darkest places.

Dr. King once wrote, "Darkness cannot drive out darkness, only light can do that. Hate cannot drive out hate, only love can do that." He poetically described the opposites of love and hate in terms of light and darkness. Acting from love instead of responding to racism with hate and fear was the foundation of his strategy. Dr. King wanted to usher in an honest peace. That's why he taught *nonviolent civil disobedience*. He led protesters to peacefully march, protest, and break unjust laws, all while bravely bearing any violence without striking back.

NONVIOLENT CIVIL DISOBEDIENCE: using peaceful actions to break laws that are viewed as wrong

---

Dr. King believed the Bible's promise that God's loving light held the power to transform oppressors into neighbors. Dr. King said, "We hope we can act in the struggle in such a way that they will see the error of their approach and will come to respect us. Then we can all live together in peace and equality."

In Montgomery, Black people were treated worse because of the color of their skin. Can you picture living like that? Black people had to use the back doors of businesses and White people's houses. They couldn't touch merchandise in stores to try on shoes or clothes. They couldn't use the same public restrooms as White people. Segregation laws forced Black people to live, learn, worship, play, and work only in places that White people allowed. The segregation laws had a name: *Jim Crow*, a derogatory name for a Black person.

Nonviolent civil disobedience against segregation was costly. During the bus boycott, Dr. King was stopped by police multiple times. He was fined for made-up traffic violations and threatened with jail. "It is an honor to face jail for a just cause," Dr. King responded. Protesters were stopped by police for riding in carpools. Black taxi drivers were harassed. Many Black protesters were fired when their White employers found out the workers were part of the boycott. A lot of white people feared *integration* because they considered Black people to have less value.

INTEGRATION: people of different races living together in freedom and equality

CIVIL RIGHTS: the rights given to citizens of a country

Even though Black Americans were citizens of the United States, they did not have the rights of citizens, called *civil rights*. The legal court with the most power, the Supreme Court, ruled that separating Black people was a fair practice. In a case called *Plessy v. Ferguson* in 1896, the Supreme Court said that "separate but equal" schools, bathrooms, neighborhoods, and shops were good for the country.

But nothing was truly equal. Black people could not vote. They did not have access to the same opportunities and power as other US citizens. In the United States, every citizen has a right to vote and have leaders who represent them in the government. But before the Voting Rights Act of 1965 became law, Black people were not represented at all. White people decided what laws would pass. White people were the judges and jurors in court. White people decided how much to spend on neighborhood schools. White people defined where it was legal and illegal for Black people to live. White people were in charge of college admissions. White people ran most hospitals and all police precincts. Black people had no voice and few choices in shaping their own lives. This divided system was based in *white supremacy*.

WHITE SUPREMACY: the belief that White people are superior to all other races

The darkness of racism and injustice was deep. The civil rights movement shone a great light on the evil of the unjust Jim Crow laws. Dr. King led movements to right the wrongs of inequality when it came to laws, voting rights, education access, and other civil rights for Black people. But he didn't stop there. He also spoke up against war, called for help for poor people, and fought racism against Latinos, Asians, Native Americans, and Jewish people. He worked to shine God's light on the dignity of all people.

Dr. King and freedom fighters of all ages and backgrounds sacrificed greatly to shine that light during the civil rights movement. Some were even prepared to give their lives. Over forty people did. Martin Luther King Jr. was killed on April 4, 1968, as he was planning a march to help sanitation workers receive fair pay. The day before, April 3, he talked about death almost as if he knew it was coming. But he was not afraid.

Well, I don't know what will happen now. We've got some difficult days ahead. But it doesn't matter with me now. . . . I just want to do God's will. And He's allowed me to go up to the mountain.

And I've looked over. And I've seen the promised land. I may not get there with you. But I want you to know tonight, that we, as a people, will get to the promised land. And so I'm happy, tonight. I'm not worried about anything. I'm not fearing any man. Mine eyes have seen the glory of the coming of the Lord!

Though Dr. King died, his light still shines. It still shines because it wasn't just Dr. King's light. It is the light of Jesus. And if we follow Jesus, His light shines in us too.

1 A LIGHT FOR ALL TO SEE

You are the world's light—a city on a hill, glowing in the night for all to see.
—MATTHEW 5:14 TLB

Darkness cannot drive out darkness, only light can do that. Hate cannot drive out hate, only love can do that.

DR. KING HURRIED THROUGH THE NIGHT. His wife and children were waiting at home for him. He looked forward to his sons' and daughter's excited cries when he walked through the door and to the warm meal in the kitchen. Beyond the street, shadows loomed. Was someone watching him? Dr. King followed the path of the streetlights that brightened his way and soon arrived home.

Like a streetlight helps us see when it is dark outside, Dr. King encouraged people to shine God's light and love for others to see—just like Jesus said in Matthew 5:14. Jesus taught that kindness and peace brighten our dark world. Violence is dark. It will only grow darker when answered with more violence. Hate is dark. It will never be beaten by dark, hate-filled words or actions. But love is a bright light. Love is welcoming, kind, and helpful. It brings people together. Like light and darkness, love and hate can't both be in control. One will be stronger.

Dr. King chose to be a light for Jesus. He shone by preaching about God's love. He encouraged people to love their neighbors. He protested unjust laws. He spoke up for the rights of all people. And like God, he accepted people of different races and cultures.

With God's help, you can drive out the darkness of evil as Jesus did in His time on earth, and as He did through Dr. King. Here are a few ways to act and speak to brighten the world:

- Be the first to apologize and to accept apologies from others.
- Keep being a friend when you're mad at someone.
- Accept people from different races, cultures, and abilities as they are—created by God as unique individuals.
- Be kind to everyone at your school and in your neighborhood.
- Stand up to bullying.
- Pray about the problems you see and for the hurting people you meet.

Being light in dark places will make you stick out, like a glowing city on a hill. Some people won't like that about you. Others will want to be near your brilliance. Let your light—your love for Jesus—shine every day. The world needs you. Shine so people can see the path of love and peace.

You can drive out darkness with light powered by God's Spirit.

Lord, help me be the light that shows others Your love. Show me peaceful ways to create change.

2 AS GOOD AS ANYONE

But if you are treating one person as if he were more important than another, then you are sinning. . . . You are guilty of breaking God's law.
—JAMES 2:9

You are as good as anyone.
(quoting his mother, Alberta Williams King)

YOUNG MARTIN PEERED AT THE MARBLE on the sidewalk. He took aim. *Tap.* His friend squealed as Martin's yellow marble passed just next to his own green one. A miss!

Martin loved playing with his friend. His friend's parents owned the store across the street, so he spent lots of time playing in Martin's yard. But when they both started school, things began to change. His friend wasn't as friendly anymore. Then when Martin was six, his friend told Martin he couldn't play with him anymore. Martin's friend was White.

Martin was sad and confused. At dinner that evening, he asked his parents about it. Martin learned about racism that day. Pastor King and Mrs. King explained America's history of treating Black people like they were worth less than White people. White people were taught not to be friends with Black people or else they would be treated just as badly.

They told Martin about slavery and segregation. He was already aware that Black people could not do the same things as White people. He knew Black people were treated unfairly. Now he knew why.

Martin felt angry. He was convinced he would spend the rest of his life hating White people.

As the meal cooled on their plates, Martin's mother promised him that being born Black did not make him less valuable. "She made it clear that she opposed this system and that I must never allow it to make me feel inferior," he later wrote. His parents said that Christians did not practice hate but had a calling to love. Little Martin eventually grew into a man with a great capacity for both love and self-respect.

Many things in life can make you feel unimportant. You might feel like you aren't able to do what God wants you to do. Maybe you think

everyone has a talent except you. Maybe you think someone is smarter. Or maybe you just feel small. Remember that God created you with your own gifts and interests for a purpose. He has jobs for you to do, and He will give you the words, skills, and courage to do them. You are not less than anyone else. You are the best *you* God could make.

Treat everyone with respect— including yourself.

Lord, thank You for making me as I am.

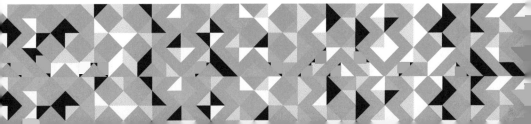

3 HOLD ON TO DIGNITY

But the voice said to him again, "God has made these things clean. Don't call them 'unholy'!"
—ACTS 10:15

They came to see that it was ultimately more honorable to walk the streets in dignity than to ride the buses in humiliation.

IN THE 1950s, riding the bus in Montgomery, Alabama, was an awful experience for Black people. They had to pay the bus fare in the front of the bus. Then they had to get off and enter the bus again through the back door. There was a section of the bus in the back for Black people—they couldn't choose where to sit. And if the bus filled up, Black people were expected to give up their seats for White people and stand.

Dr. King became a pastor in 1954 in Montgomery. He had lived there for a year when Rosa Parks refused to let a White passenger take her seat on a bus. She disobeyed the law that allowed segregation on buses, and she was arrested.

Black residents were tired of being treated as if they had no worth. After Rosa's arrest, they decided to boycott the buses. Beginning December 5, 1955, they did not take buses anywhere. They chose Dr. King to be the spokesperson for the boycott. Through this event, he became a nationally known civil rights leader.

Most Black people in Montgomery did not have access to cars. They walked to jobs, to church, to buy groceries. Some workers were fired for participating in the boycott. Some were arrested and put in jail. But even with all of these sacrifices, Black people stayed off the buses.

The city found out exactly how much Black customers were worth: they lost 30,000–40,000 fares per day, every day for over a year. The boycott ended after 381 days on December 20, 1956, when the city removed segregated seating. That same year, the Supreme Court ruled against segregated busing. The Black people of Montgomery maintained their dignity.

In the Bible's book of Acts, the apostle Peter looked down on Gentiles. He thought they were worth less than Jewish people like him. But God came to him in a dream to tell him that Gentiles were equal to Jews. He directed Peter to welcome Gentiles into the family of God. When Peter woke up, three Gentiles showed up at his door. Peter quickly realized God wanted him to go with the men. Peter's obedience led to many people becoming Christians.

God created humans in His image (Genesis 1:27), so we should feel worthy! Living under segregation laws stripped dignity from Black people. When the people of Montgomery were fed up with their worth being challenged, they fought back. When you encounter people who try to strip you or others of dignity, fight back with truth.

Fight for the worth of all people.

Dear God, thank You for fighting to preserve our worth.

4 OWN IT

Yes, God is working in you to help you want to do what pleases him. Then he gives you the power to do it.
—PHILIPPIANS 2:13

We were inspired with a desire to give to our young a true sense of their own stake in freedom and justice. We believed they would have the courage to respond to our call.

CHILDREN STREAMED THROUGH THE DOORS of the church. Girls, boys, and teenagers chattered about the classes they would be missing and their parents' reactions to their plans. Some parents warned their children to stay in school and not go to the church. Other parents cried, smiled, and prayed over their children.

The youth entering the Sixteenth Street Baptist Church in Birmingham had come to march.

When protests in Birmingham stalled because Black adults were afraid, the civil rights leaders decided to ask children to help. Kids couldn't be fired from jobs or thrown out of rented homes. Dr. King and the other leaders believed young people could have a big impact.

Dr. King expected criticism for encouraging children to protest. But he felt they needed to be part of the solution to segregation. He trusted that they would do a good job. And he believed they would have the needed courage. Dr. King was right! The Birmingham Children's Crusade led to a frenzy of news coverage and a national demand for civil rights for Black people. The campaign was key in pressuring the government to pass the Civil Rights Act of 1964 and outlaw segregation.

Over one thousand young people marched toward Birmingham's downtown on May 2, 1963. Hundreds ended up in jail. Still, the next day, hundreds more children and teens joined another march. It was scary. Police yelled through megaphones, "Get out of this line, or you're going to jail." When the young marchers continued, the police did not hold back. One participant later remembered: "First we were faced with the dogs and the water hoses. . . . They kick out a hundred pounds of pressure. They tore clothes and tore flesh. . . . We were put

in a cellblock [that] I understand holds 650 people. And this cellblock had over 1,500 people there. There were so many people there."

Photographs of police attacking the children appeared across the country. The young faces staring down water hoses, growling dogs, and police batons had an impact that the same images of adults had not had. People across the country and around the world were horrified at the brutality and awakened to the cruelty of white supremacy.

But the news coverage also revealed the courage of the children. They showed more strength than the cowardly adults who hurt and jailed them. Their brave actions helped push segregation toward extinction. They experienced the vast problems of their community, and they decided to be part of the solution. They did not wait until they grew up to demand justice.

It's great to work toward a world that's fair for other people. But you can also do it for yourself. You deserve justice and kindness. Own it! And when you build yourself a better future, you also create change for others.

Stand up for yourself.

Holy Spirit, please help me draw on God's power as I defend my own worth.

AUDREY FAYE HENDRICKS

May 22, 1953–March 1, 2009

Audrey Faye Hendricks was only nine years old, but she knew her legs could keep up on the march. One spring morning in 1963, she strode to church in Birmingham, Alabama. A group of children were gathering for a march. She had dressed for the special day, wearing shiny patent leather shoes, a crisp white top, and a pretty pink sweater. She was willing to go to jail.

Audrey lined up with other children. She was the only student from her elementary school, but she didn't mind. She was ready to walk along with hundreds of older kids. The children were marching to protest segregation. She was young, but she already knew what it was like to drink from a dirty water fountain and sit at the back of the bus.

On May 2, more than one thousand children and teens marched. They sang "Ain't Gonna Let Nobody Turn Me 'Round." Audrey was the youngest marcher. Even though they were just children, Audrey and many other marchers were arrested. Audrey stayed in jailed for six long days. Angry jail guards shouted at her, and she was surrounded by strangers. She was also locked up in a tiny room all by herself for many hours. Audrey became one of the youngest people to get arrested during the civil rights movement. Hundreds of children were jailed by the end of what became known as the Children's Crusade.

5 THE DREAM

Now, in Christ, there is no difference between Jew and Greek. There is no difference between slaves and free men. There is no difference between male and female. You are all the same in Christ Jesus.
—GALATIANS 3:28

I still have a dream . . . that one day this nation will rise up and live out the true meaning of its creed: "We hold these truths to be self-evident, that all men are created equal."

DR. KING FACED 250,000 PEOPLE packed into the National Mall, with the Washington Monument towering in the background. A sea of Black and White people, Catholics and Protestants, Jews and Gentiles had joined the march in support of Black people at the 1963 March for Jobs and Freedom in Washington, DC. Dr. King had worked for days on his speech for the march. He was still laboring over it in his hotel the night before and finally finished writing at 4 a.m. It was good, but there was something missing.

When the time for the speech arrived, Dr. King started reading. His friend Mahalia Jackson was sitting nearby. She didn't recognize the usual fire in Dr. King's words. She leaned toward the podium and whispered, "Tell them about the dream, Martin." Her encouragement brought Dr. King back to himself. He put down the speech he had worked on so long and said the now famous words: "I still have a dream." Energy surged through his voice as he talked freely from his heart.

Dr. King's dream was that America would treat everyone as equal, as the Constitution says. He believed that the Constitution echoed the truth of the Bible. The apostle Paul wrote about equality in Christ because he observed that Jewish believers didn't think Gentiles (non-Jews) could be acceptable to Jesus unless they followed Jewish rules. Jewish believers separated themselves because they felt they were closer to God. Paul corrected that view. He told them that in Christ, all believers are united in love. They were equal even if they were not the same.

Dr. King's speech was aired on television. Newspapers wrote about it. People around the world loved it! The speech quickly became one of the most famous speeches ever delivered. People still quote from it today. Dr. King's "I Have a Dream" speech is so loved, because his vision of everyone getting along was so beautiful.

Just like Dr. King needed a little reminder to share his dream, you can remember the truth behind that dream: we were all created equal by a God who loves each of us. When we celebrate our uniqueness and respect each other—both for our differences and our similarities—we are living the dream.

Make friends with someone who is different from you.

Holy Spirit, remind me of the beauty of being diverse yet unified in Jesus.

6 WHAT ARE WE WORTH?

To God every person is the same.
—ACTS 10:34

Human worth lies in relatedness to God. An individual has value because he has value to God. Whenever this is recognized, "whiteness" and "blackness" pass away . . . and "son" and "brother" are substituted.

"TIME FOR CLASS!" MRS. JANE ELLIOTT CALLED to the third graders. Before the school day began, Mrs. Elliott wanted to make some special rules. On this day, blue-eyed boys and girls would be the first to eat, first to go to recess, and would be allowed to drink from the water fountain. "Brown-eyed children must use paper cups. They cannot touch the fountain," she said.

Mrs. Elliott wanted to demonstrate the injustice of prejudice. She wanted to show her students that people all have the same value, and they should not be segregated based on a physical feature.

Eventually, both the brown-eyed kids and the blue-eyed kids experienced being treated unfairly and treating their classmates unfairly.

A few truths came from this lesson:

- Mistreating people because of a physical feature doesn't make sense.

- It is easy to become the person who mistreats another.
- People feel small when they are mistreated because of a physical feature.
- When one group treats another group as less valuable, both groups suffer.

God does not treat people better or worse because of any feature—not their money, where they live, where they go to school, or what kind of devices they have. God does not treat people differently depending on their skin color either. His love is too big to be limited! Every human is made in the image of God. This alone gives every one of us worth. When we hurt or make fun of other people because of how God made them, we are disagreeing with God.

Dr. King based his civil rights actions on what he knew about God. He knew that God valued all people and that we are born with worth simply because God made us and loves us. Dr. King believed that the officers who hauled him to jail were valuable to God, just as much as he believed that his own children were valuable to God.

Peace comes when we honor everyone's God-made differences and understand that we are all loved and valued by God.

God loves you—a lot. And God loves your neighbors, your classmates, your relatives, and even your enemies.

Know your worth. Know your neighbor's worth.

Holy Spirit, help me treat everyone with the same love—Yours.

7 DON'T BE AFRAID

 "So don't be afraid of those people. Everything that is hidden will be shown. Everything that is secret will be made known."
—MATTHEW 10:26

 Our fears assume many different disguises and dress themselves in strangely different robes.

AFTER THE CIVIL WAR ENDED in 1865, many White people were afraid of what would happen now that Blacks were free. How would farmers make a living without unpaid labor? Who would care for the children and clean homes? Would Black people take jobs and land away from White people?

In Tennessee, a group of White people encouraged these fears, and they spread racist ideas that Black people were not fully human. This group called themselves the Ku Klux Klan (KKK). As they spread a culture of hate across the South and the country, the group became a coordinated organization with members, leaders, and meetings. Klan members were White business owners, church leaders, bankers, and others community leaders. They attacked Black people and their property and poisoned Black life with constant fear. Klan members did not want people to know that they were part of the group, so they hid behind white robes and white hoods.

Today, there are a few white supremacist groups that continue the KKK's mission of fear and racist hate. They claim that Black people and other people of color are inferior to White people. Their goal is to keep people of color from enjoying equal rights as Americans. Other people, who aren't part of any official group, spread fear and hate from secret shadows too: The bully who picks on the kid with clothes from the thrift store when the teacher isn't looking. The person with a fake online profile who writes angry posts. The news reporter who twists the facts to support or attack a certain group or person.

There are plenty of things to be afraid of in this world. But God says we don't need to fear. He sees the faces and hearts of these bullies in the shadows. He will pull off their masks and robes and expose their secrets.

Is there someone who makes you feel afraid? Ask God to give you courage and help you know the best way to respond. Talk to an adult you trust about the situation. They might help you see a way to expose the hate and stop it. Or they might help you overcome your fears and ignore the bully. But no matter how scary things look, remember that God is by your side.

Memorize a Bible verse about courage.

*Holy Spirit, expose wrongdoing, and help
me trust You when I am afraid.*

8 SEE THE BEAUTY

There were so many people that no one could count them. They were from every nation, tribe, people, and language of the earth. They were all standing before the throne and before the Lamb.
—REVELATION 7:9

Unity has never meant uniformity.

WHAT COLOR IS YOUR HAIR? What color are your eyes? Are they an exact match of your relatives' or friends' features? Do the differences make you love those people less? Of course not!

Differences are good to our Creator. God designed the world to be full of color. Flowers, trees, and people show God's plan for a diverse world. When people of many cultures are together, you can see God's handiwork. He made people with pale skin. He made other people with darker shades. And God did not stop there. He created different eye shapes and colors. Even hair ranges in color from very light to very dark.

Maybe you've heard well-meaning people say, "I don't see color." It's a way they express acceptance of people of different races. They try to be "color-blind." But while it sounds like a celebration of people's sameness, it's more like erasing their uniqueness. Color is everywhere. You can't miss it. Can you imagine someone not seeing your skin, hair, or eye color? It's hard to think how that would work. Would you look like a skeleton? Would all the colorful parts of you be invisible?

God created a diversity in texture, color, size, sound, and taste. He didn't want us to ignore these differences! That is why God gave us senses to experience all the diversity that the world has to offer. This is not only true here but in heaven.

In the book of Revelation, the author describes a scene of worship in front of God's heavenly throne. He describes the worshipers by what they have in common and by their differences. They all loved God and wanted to shout about being saved. But they did not look or sound the same at all. They didn't worship in one language, but in *every* language. Heaven does not erase where people come from. Our differences are a beautiful part of worship.

The world is beautiful *because* of its diversity. See the beauty in people, just how God made them. Be accepting. Try to be a bridge that connects different people. Help people see how much God loves them and how wonderfully He made them.

Enjoy God's colorful world.

Holy Spirit, help me fully accept people so they feel seen and heard.

9 KNOWN BY LOVE

 "Love each other as I have loved you. All people will know that you are my followers if you love each other."
—JOHN 13:34–35 NCV

 The aftermath of nonviolence is the creation of the beloved community, while the aftermath of violence is tragic bitterness.

DR. AND MRS. KING STEPPED OFF the plane. They had been traveling for many hours and were tired but excited. They were in India! They toured there for an entire month to learn more about *satyagraha* (suht YAH gruh huh).

Dr. King had read about one of India's most well-loved citizens, Mohandas Gandhi. Gandhi had defined satyagraha as "truth force" or "holding on to truth" and fought the inequality and discrimination in his country based on this idea. At the time, some Indians were called "untouchable," the bottom of a ranking system that separated Indians. The "untouchables" were blocked from education and worship. They were trapped in poverty.

Gandhi refused to call people "untouchable" and instead called them "children of God." He took rejected people into the temples to worship by his side. He also resisted British control. The British government had taken India away from the people by force decades earlier, and Gandhi didn't think the way they treated Indians was right. Gandhi wanted to build a nation where all people were valued. Though Gandhi had died years before the Kings' visit, his principles were alive.

Dr. King carried the tool of satyagraha back to America. He envisioned a world powered by love and empty of discrimination, poverty, and violence. He called this world the "Beloved Community," and he believed that peace would come when everyone solved conflicts through love instead of violence.

As leaders, Gandhi and King were willing to suffer for righteous justice: they were both arrested, received death threats, and were killed for their activism.

Jesus said that the greatest love people could show was to lay down their lives for their friends (John 15:13). Dr. King imagined a Beloved Community where every member would have the same willingness to sacrifice out of love. His vision came directly from Jesus. Jesus could have chosen any godly characteristic for his disciples to focus on, but he chose "love each other" as the way to show that we belong to Him.

Can you imagine this community? A place where people of all races and abilities live together with love and respect. A place where people settle disagreements with handshakes and where kind words are frequent and people honor differences. A place where everyone has food, medicine, housing, and education. Now imagine if that kind of harmony and security existed in communities all over the world.

Let your love for others be the biggest building block in the Beloved Community.

Build the Beloved Community by responding to problems with love and respect.

God, may the way I treat others show Your great love.

10 ALL TOGETHER NOW

 Let us think about each other and help each other to show love and do good deeds.
—HEBREWS 10:24

 Injustice anywhere is a threat to justice everywhere. ... Whatever affects one directly, affects all indirectly.

"I AM IN BIRMINGHAM because injustice is here."

In a letter written from a jail cell in 1963, Dr. King explained why he had come to Alabama. He had just led one thousand people through town without a parade permit. Some people wished he would leave. They complained that Alabama was turning into an uncomfortable place to live because outsiders were coming to the state to protest. They thought that Black people were content with segregation, no representation, and being treated as less than human. These people accused Dr. King of bringing racial unrest to a peaceful place.

This was not true! In fact, only those complaining people were comfortable with racism. They didn't notice the burning crosses, the murders, the unemployment, and the limited housing that their Black neighbors suffered. They didn't notice that racism had made their state into a place of constant violence. They didn't notice because their hearts were blind to injustice.

Racism hurts everyone. Black people were the victims of racial violence, but White people were also damaged. They limited their own humanity by the ways they treated other people as less. They got used to the way of violence. This is what Dr. King meant when he said, "Whatever affects one directly, affects all indirectly." We are all part of one community.

A *network* is a system connecting things or people. The civil rights movement was a justice network created to stop the violent network of racism. The movement included all kinds of people who understood that human rights for Black people would improve the entire country. They understood that the fight for equal rights benefits everyone.

In the book of Hebrews, the author talked about the importance of encouraging one another. Following Jesus means understanding that believers are connected in one faith community. We are connected to the people in the past who showed faith in God. We are connected to people in the present, too, for mutual support.

You get to decide what kind of network you want to be part of. Will you pause your life to help people in need and encourage others to join you?

Stand up for justice, anywhere and everywhere.

Lord, give me eyes to see the network of love, and join it.

RUBY BRIDGES

September 8, 1954–

Every step took six-year-old Ruby Bridges closer to the front doors of her new school. She walked with her mother between four police officers as objects flew toward them. Grown-ups yelled ugly words. Ruby gripped her mother's hand. She was too scared to cry. She walked straight into the school.

Ruby was one of the first Black students to integrate an all-White school in the United States. She had gone to kindergarten at an all-Black school, but when she was in first grade, segregation became illegal. Black and White children could now go to school together. The new school was closer to Ruby's home. The building was nicer. The books were newer. So, in 1960, Ruby's parents decided to send her to William Frantz Elementary School in New Orleans. She was the only Black student enrolled.

The White students and their parents didn't want Ruby there. A crowd gathered outside the school to tell little Ruby to stay out. Special officers called federal marshals kept Ruby safe. For an entire year, Ruby was the only student in her class, because the other children's

The next year, some of the White children returned. And there were other Black children at the school too. Ruby had classmates to play with! Ruby, her parents, and other courageous families braved angry crowds and violence to integrate schools. Because of their actions, children of all colors can play and learn together.

11 WORK TOGETHER

 Whoever spends time with wise people will become wise. But whoever makes friends with fools will suffer.
—PROVERBS 13:20

 We must all learn to live together as brothers, or we will all perish together as fools.

PEOPLE FLOWED INTO CHRIST CHURCH CATHEDRAL. They pressed against a steady wind to make it on time, clutching hats in place. Over one thousand St. Louis residents packed into the church. They stood wherever they could find space as sleeves and handbags brushed and bumped. Those lucky enough to sit perched on folding chairs that were placed up to the altar. As clouds gathered and thickened outside, the ushers closed the doors to the packed church. Hundreds of disappointed people returned home.

The crowd had come to hear Dr. King.

As he began to speak that day in March 1964, the people fell silent and still. Dr. King's voice filled the room.

"God is interested in the freedom of the whole human race," he said. He argued that a civil rights law, which was in progress, would be for everyone. Americans could live together in love like one big family, or they could all suffer the consequences of racist foolishness.

Racism affects everybody. It hurts its victims in obvious ways, scarring bodies and limiting opportunities. But racism also hurts the people who believe they are better because of their skin color. Hate fills their hearts. They do terrible things. They also miss out on the friendships and knowledge that other people offer. Racists are fools!

The civil rights movement revealed the foolishness of segregation. Business owners refused services to Black people even though it meant losing money. Schools shut down instead of letting Black students attend. Loving mothers turned into screaming bullies as they yelled threats and insults at Black children entering their children's schools. The hate of racism poisoned their hearts and souls.

Dr. King called on everyone to come together in love and move

forward to create an America that acted like one big family of brothers and sisters. If they didn't, the whole country would suffer the punishment of fools.

Who is a wise person you know? What advice or assistance from a parent, teacher, coach, or friend has helped you love in bigger and better ways? Maybe you've experienced some foolishness when you followed a bad piece of advice or bad example. Don't be a fool! Join with wise people who show love and treat everyone like family.

Ask God for wisdom.

Holy Spirit, I'm sorry for times I've acted as a fool by treating others badly. Help me grow in wisdom.

12 OPEN YOUR EYES

"Don't be afraid," the prophet answered. "Those who are with us are more than those who are with them." And Elisha prayed, "Open his eyes, LORD, so that he may see."
—2 KINGS 6:16–17 NIV

Let us remember that there is a creative force in this universe working to pull down the gigantic mountains of evil, a power that is able to make a way out of no way and transform dark yesterdays into bright tomorrows.

AN UNLIKELY ARMY WAS FORMING. College students crowded into the plaza—some even sat on the roofs of courtyard buildings. Some young people road-tripped from other parts of California just to hear Dr. King's speech about the war in Vietnam. As he looked out into the crowd of young people, Dr. King must have noticed that almost all of them were White, and all were listening with focus.

"It costs $500,000 to kill every enemy soldier while we spend only $53 a year for every poor person," King said. The students were afraid of being forced to serve in the army. They did not agree with the war and did not see the Vietnamese as their enemies. These young people reflected the kind of "army" Dr. King hoped for: an army of love, with troops who desired to seek good for their neighbors locally and globally.

God is always on the side of goodness, justice, and love. Whenever we stand up for these causes, we don't stand alone. God is with us.

Often, God also uses people to bring about justice and love—allies arrive from unexpected places. In Dr. King's case, those allies were young White students. Dr. King had the vision to recognize how these young people were affected by war policies, and the young people had the vision to recognize Dr. King as a leader worth listening to.

We cannot always see the vision of justice and change that God works to bring into the world. Sometimes we can only see our problems. Sometimes we can only see how strong and scary the other side looks. This was the case for Elisha's servant.

Elisha was one of the Old Testament prophets. His role was to speak to the Israelites as God told him and to do what God empowered him to do. At the time, the Arameans were at war with the Israelites and had surrounded the city where Elisha was in order to capture him. Elisha's servant was afraid. But Elisha trusted God and was not afraid. Elisha prayed for his servant to see what he could see: the army of God with chariots of fire surrounding the enemy.

When we are doing the work of God—telling the truth, showing kindness, defending right—we don't have to be afraid. God is already there, fighting with us. He has our back when we are doing His will.

Talk to others about what God is doing in your community.

Holy Spirit, show me where You are working so I can join You.

13 FACE OF THE FUTURE

My friends, as believers in our Lord Jesus Christ, the Lord of glory, you must never treat people in different ways according to their outward appearance.
—JAMES 2:1 GNT

You young people . . . have somehow discovered the central fact of American life—that the extension of democracy for all Americans depends upon complete integration of Negro Americans.

DR. KING LOOKED OVER THE CROWD before he delivered his speech. He was pleased that 26,000 young people had marched in Washington, DC. Before him stood youth ranging in age from elementary school kids to college students. Their faces were all hues, as dark as the night sky, golden brown, and light as cream. Civil rights leaders and other citizens also joined the crowd in the 1959 Youth March for Integrated Schools. It was the second march to show support for school integration, allowing children from all races to go to school together.

School integration was moving slowly in the 1950s. It had been five years since the Supreme Court decided that separate schools due to race was unlawful in a case called *Brown v. Board of Education*. But state governments hadn't changed the practice of having separate schools for White and Black children. Many southern states closed schools instead of welcoming Black students to join their White peers in the classroom.

In front of Dr. King that day were 26,000 reasons why integration was a priority for the youth. The young people at the march showed that they were serious about the court's ruling becoming a reality in their schools. Not only that, but as Dr. King looked at the energetic crowd, he saw the potential of new voters who could shift the positions of Congress and the president with their votes.

Dr. King and other civil rights leaders organized youth marches to put pressure on the states to obey the law and end segregation in education. Dr. King also wanted to show the Supreme Court justices that many people supported them. He invited citizens who were northerners and southerners, young and old, Black and White to march to show support for the court's decision.

Dr. King called this crowd the "face of the future," a future where children of different races would learn and grow and play together. He saw their unity. He admired their courage and their commitment to democracy.

Today, you are the face of the future. How will you bring unity and equality to your world?

Find a way to make your school a better place for all kids to learn.

Holy Spirit, thank You for the people who help me learn.

14 GOD IS WORKING

 And this hope will never disappoint us, because God has poured out his love to fill our hearts.
—ROMANS 5:5

 We shall overcome because the arc of the moral universe is long but it bends toward justice.

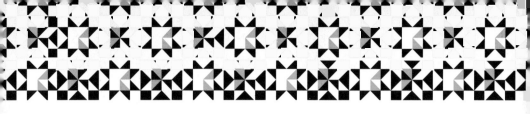

VOICES ROSE TOGETHER, high and low, young and old:

Oh, deep in my heart, I do believe
We shall overcome some day.

As the song "We Shall Overcome" continued, the voices gained strength and filled the church. The guitar strummed in double time. Feet stamped. Hands clapped.

Black people have always used music to build community. Enslaved Africans sang religious songs, called *spirituals*, to call on God's strength and hope. Sometimes the songs included hidden messages about escaping to freedom. Other songs announced secret meetings. Some songs were heartfelt prayers of pain and pleading. After slavery, Black people passed the songs down to their children and grandchildren. They sang to celebrate their heritage. They sang to protest unfair treatment. They sang to worship.

Many spirituals transformed into freedom songs during the civil rights movement. Activists sang at planning meetings, at sit-ins, and on marches. Sometimes they added new words about current challenges. Like the melodies of their ancestors, the notes and lyrics of freedom songs gave activists strength. Singing together also created unity and encouraged the people to keep working together.

Freedom songs also flooded people with hope. Songs helped people trust God in hard situations. Songs like "We Shall Overcome" voiced a confidence in a better future. Dr. King especially liked the song because it echoed his belief that good would defeat evil. He believed Black people would overcome the struggles they faced in

America. And he hoped nonviolent resistance would help Black and White people work toward this future together.

Romans 5 mentions hope that does not disappoint. The only hope that does not disappoint is hope based on a mighty God. God keeps His promises. We can't see all that He is doing. But we can believe that He is working. Trust in God. "This hope will never disappoint" you. He shall overcome.

Write a note encouraging someone to hope in God.

Holy Spirit, help me face difficulty with a hopeful heart.

SHEYANN WEBB

February 17, 1956—

"If you can't vote, then you're not free; and if you ain't free, children, then you're a slave." Eight-year-old Sheyann Webb remembered the words she had heard in church. She was afraid, but gripping the hand of a teacher and singing gave her courage to keep walking.

> *Ain't gonna let nobody turn me 'round.*
> *I'm gonna keep on a-walkin', keep on a-talkin',*
> *Marchin' down to freedom land.*

Sheyann was marching for voting rights with hundreds of other Black people in Selma, Alabama, that day in March 1965. They were protesting the laws and violence that stopped Black people from voting. It was a scary day that became known as "Bloody Sunday." Police attacked the participants. Some were jailed. Sheyann got pushed around, but she was not hurt or arrested.

A couple months before the march, Sheyann had seen a crowd going into Brown Chapel AME Church. Black *and* White people were walking up the steps together! Sheyann never saw *that* in segregated Alabama. She was curious, and she went inside.

The group had gathered to plan events to get Black people to sign up to vote. Sheyann heard about the power of voting. She heard preacher Hosea Williams talk about how being barred from voting was like slavery. Sheyann eagerly got involved. She attended more meetings, often leading the group in freedom songs.

Dr. King made friends with Sheyann and played games with her. He called her the "smallest freedom fighter." As an adult, Sheyann remembered how she and other children marched. "We were just ordinary kids who wanted freedom," she said.

15 HOPE THROUGH THE HARD

 So let's not get tired of doing what is good. At just the right time we will reap a harvest of blessing if we don't give up.
—GALATIANS 6:9 NLT

 Their death says to us that we must work passionately and unrelentingly for the realization of the American dream.

THE CHURCH WAS ALIVE with the hustle and bustle of a Sunday morning. Churchgoers wore crisp suits and ties and beautiful, big hats and dresses in pastel colors. Young boys mimicked the dress of their fathers, with bright white dress shirts and dark dress pants. Little girls wore their hair in curls that bounced as they ran in shiny patent leather shoes down to the basement just before service. The young people gathered to prepare. They were excited to celebrate Youth Day. They would be leading prayer, singing, and preaching that day.

The Sixteenth Street Baptist Church in Birmingham was not only a place of worship, but a planning place for civil rights activities. Church members would worship, then hit the streets to march. They participated in sit-ins and other nonviolent action. Its pastor was passionate about fighting injustice. Its downtown location was easy to get to. And it quickly became the place for freedom fighters to attend meetings.

Sixteenth Street Baptist Church faced a lot of resistance because of its fight for justice in Birmingham. It received a lot of threats. Then came September 15, 1963. Churchgoers were attending Sunday school before morning service. At 10:22 a.m., a bomb struck the church. Four girls—14-year-olds Addie Mae Collins, Cynthia Wesley, and Carole Robertson and 11-year-old Denise McNair—were killed while attending Sunday school. More than twenty other people were hurt.

The bombing did not stop the church, however. Shocked by the attack, people from around the world gave money to restore the church building. Black people in Birmingham kept coming to the church and organizing protests, even as they mourned the loss of those precious girls. The members of Sixteenth Street Baptist Church did not let terrorism stop them. They continued to serve the God of freedom. They continued to pray, trust God, and show up.

Remaining hopeful is hard some days. But don't give up. Don't run away. Show up with God's people and keep doing His work.

Don't let the dark clouds dim your light.

*Holy Spirit, help me keep working
when bad things happen.*

16 DON'T GO LOW

 Do not let evil defeat you. Defeat evil by doing good.
—ROMANS 12:21

 Let no man pull you so low as to hate him.

DR. KING'S WIFE, CORETTA, CALLED HIM with good news: he was going to receive the Nobel Peace Prize for 1964! Dr. King was stunned. He knew he was nominated for the international award, but he had not stopped to think about the possibility of winning.

In his autobiography, Dr. King wrote that the award was not because of his work alone. He gave a shout-out to the thousands of people involved in the civil rights movement. He wrote, "These are the real heroes of the freedom struggle: they are the noble people for whom I accept the Nobel Peace Prize."

The Nobel Peace Prize is given to honor peacemakers around the world. Dr. King was chosen for the award because he dedicated his life to fighting hate with love. He always reminded people that love could lead to peace. He challenged people to avoid acting like their haters. If they did, hate would defeat them. Hate would bring them low.

For Dr. King and the freedom fighters, the Nobel Prize confirmed they were doing the right thing. It told them that continuing their peaceful protests, despite much hate and violence, mattered to the whole world. They had endured beatings from police and dirty jail cells. They had endured the church bombing that killed four little girls. They had endured the drive-by shooting of Medgar Evers by members of the Ku Klux Klan. They had endured the murders of Andrew Goodman, James Chaney, and Michael Schwerner, who were helping to organize voter drives in Mississippi during Freedom Summer, a coordinated effort across the South to protest for voting rights.

They had endured these things and so much more. But still they chose peaceful nonviolence. God gave them a supernatural ability to refuse to match hateful actions with more hatred. They were lights shining stubbornly in darkness.

You can't fight hate with hate. You won't solve problems by being mean to people who are mean to you. In the end, you will be brought low. You will be like the people who hate you. Don't become what you oppose. Fight evil by doing good.

Love your haters; don't be like them.

Father, please help me defeat evil through the power of Your love.

17 TEMPORARY SETBACK

So do not lose the courage that you had in the past. It has a great reward.
—HEBREWS 10:35

I believe that unarmed truth and unconditional love will have the final word in reality. This is why right, temporarily defeated, is stronger than evil triumphant.

DR. KING HELD THE HEAVY GOLD DISC. He was in Oslo, Norway, in December 1964 to accept the Nobel Peace Prize medal for his leadership in civil rights.

A medal for peace. But peace did not yet exist in America. Still, much had changed. The Civil Rights Act had finally passed that summer. Segregation was outlawed. It was now illegal in the United States to discriminate against people based on their religion, race, or gender. This was a huge moment of victory.

But though Dr. King was hopeful about the act's results, he also understood that changing the law was only one of many steps to creating a Beloved Community. Ten years after *Brown v. Board of Education*, schools were still segregated. Racists who were angry about the legal changes were becoming even more violent. Freedom Summer had resulted in many volunteers being beaten and killed.

In the midst of these continuing struggles, Dr. King accepted the Nobel Peace Prize as a symbol of hope. He trusted that nonviolent resistance and love would outlast evil. Dr. King's confidence in God allowed him to believe in an outcome some people thought could not happen.

To keep going through struggles and make a lasting difference, you need confidence in God and what He says in His Word. Trust that you are following God's light when you oppose wrongs. Remember the reward of faith—getting to see the work of God. Confident trust in the Lord is faith in action.

Dr. King encouraged his listeners not to worry about setbacks. God and good always win. Do you feel like you're moving backward in your fight for good? Read God's promises in the Bible and ask Him to help you trust Him. Then keep going! Right is always stronger than evil in the end.

Build your confidence by remembering all that God has done in the Bible and in your life.

Lord, help me trust You when I face defeat.

18 PATTERNS AND STARS

 We know that in everything God works for the good of those who love him.
—ROMANS 8:28

 When it is dark enough, you can see the stars.
(quoting historian Charles A. Beard)

A PORTRAIT OF FORMER FIRST LADY Michelle Obama hangs in the National Portrait Gallery. The painter, Amy Sherald, included clever details in the painting. She shaded the First Lady's skin a gray tone in order to move the viewer to think about the color of Mrs. Obama's skin. The dress features geometric patterns: Rectangle-shaped strips of white alternating with vibrant red, pink, and yellow. Black trading off with gray.

These patterns are similar to traditional quilt patterns from Alabama. Quilters take bits of cloth that would have been thrown away and transform them into useful blankets that are also beautiful pieces of art. Quilts are treasures made from scraps. The patterns Amy Sherald included on Mrs. Obama's dress honor the many Black women who have made a way out of no way, so they could keep their families warm and loved.

Quilting is an important craft in Black history. During slavery, owners often didn't provide for basic needs, so enslaved women gathered discarded scraps to make quilts to keep their families warm. Over the generations, women have passed down the craft of quilt-making.

One area known for quilts is Gee's Bend, Alabama. Black women in Gee's Bend continued making quilts long after slavery ended in 1865. By the time of the civil rights movement, their skills were greatly admired. Dr. King visited Gee's Bend to preach at Pleasant Grove Baptist Church in 1965. He met some of the quilters and saw their beautiful work. He encouraged them to get involved in the fight for civil rights. They joined marches for voting rights and other nonviolent action in Alabama.

Then in 1966, some of the Gee's Bend quilters started the Freedom

Quilting Bee with neighbors in Rehoboth, Alabama. The Freedom Quilting Bee helped poor women earn money to support their families. Some of the quilters even sent their kids to college with the money they earned quilting!

Quilts are one example of creativity that came out of the dark times Black people have faced. God always brings beauty out of trouble (Isaiah 61:3).

Change your mind about the darkness. You don't have to like it, but you can choose to be positive when it comes. You can trust God for the good that will happen. You can also be the star in a friend's life when they are in darkness. Bring the light of hope in God.

Stars only come out in the dark. You will miss them if you don't look up. Don't miss God's work in your life. Look up to see Him shine.

Look up when you're feeling down.

God, thank You for being near on dark days.

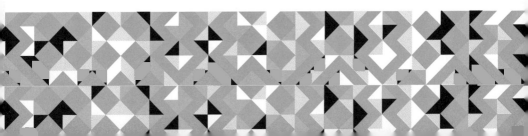

19 CHANGE IS COMING

But you should be strong. Don't give up, because you will get a reward for your good work.
—2 CHRONICLES 15:7

Go back to Mississippi, go back to Alabama, go back to South Carolina, go back to Georgia; go back to Louisiana, go back to the slums and ghettos of the northern cities, knowing that somehow this situation can and will be changed. Let us not wallow in the valley of despair.

THE MARCH ON WASHINGTON IS FAMOUS for Dr. King's "I Have a Dream" speech, but the march itself was a delayed dream for Black politician A. Philip Randolph. Mr. Randolph had the idea for a march for jobs in 1941, when Blacks weren't offered the same job opportunities as Whites in manufacturing and government during World War II. Mr. Randolph tried to work with the federal government for equal job opportunities, but nothing changed.

He didn't give up though. Years later Mr. Randolph, Dr. King, and other civil rights leaders worked together to organize the March for Jobs and Freedom.

Dr. King knew that the marchers would be fired up when they left Washington, DC, after the event. But he also knew that the harsh reality of their lives would confront them when they got back home. Many of the marchers still lived in segregated towns. They still lived in fear of violence, especially in the South. They still lived in poverty. They needed to hold on to hope for a changed future when they arrived home.

Dr. King's audience had come from different places all over the country. But they all faced the same opposition to equal rights. He addressed them as one community while also speaking directly to their different challenges. He spoke to the people living in segregated cities in southern states. He spoke to the people from poor areas in northern states. And he also talked to the people watching on television. He had the same encouragement for them all: "Let us not wallow in the valley of despair."

Change usually takes many people speaking out over many days or years. And it's okay to feel sad that wrong things don't quickly change. But keep believing in equal rights for everyone. Encourage friends who are left out and help everyone find a place to belong. And don't lose hope. Remember all the ways life improved for Black people during the years of the civil rights movement. Then think of the good you're doing now. You really are making a difference! Don't give up faith in the dream of a changed world. Hope in God's promise that your good work will be rewarded.

Hold on to your hope in God's promises.

Lord, please help me when I feel discouraged or sad.

ROBERT AVERY

August 8, 1948—

"**M**om, we're getting ready to go to Washington," Robert announced. "I need a change of clothes, and whatever money you might have."

Robert's mother let him go! Fifteen-year-old Robert and two friends walked out of Gadsden, Alabama, with ten dollars and a sign that said *Washington or Bust*. They were headed to the 1963 March on Washington. They depended on their own feet and rides from strangers.

The young men bravely walked and hitchhiked almost seven hundred miles from Gadsden to Washington, DC. It wasn't a safe route. In 1960, a civil rights protester had been killed only seven miles from Robert's house. William Moore was shot by the Ku Klux Klan, and no one was arrested for his death.

The boys shared small snacks they bought and slept in bus stations. They sometimes walked thirty miles between rides. Many different people picked them up. Some drivers were Black. But many were White, including a bus driver who gave them a free ride.

Robert and his friends got to Washington, DC, one week before the march. They helped organizers and made march signs. They even met

Dr. King. Robert's parents had managed to contact Dr. King and asked him to look for the boys. Dr. King found them while they were volunteering. He said, "I just came from your hometown and your parents want me to check on you."

Robert Avery never forgot the time he left home to march for freedom and met Martin Luther King Jr. He grew up to serve his hometown of Gadsden as an activist and a six-term member of the Gadsden City Council.

20 A BRIGHTER TOMORROW

Then wolves will live in peace with lambs. And leopards will lie down to rest with goats. Calves, lions and young bulls will eat together. And a little child will lead them.
—ISAIAH 11:6

I believe that even amid today's mortar bursts and whining bullets, there is still hope for a brighter tomorrow.

GOING TO WAR AGAINST ANOTHER NATION is not like fighting with your sister or brother. War is a series of battles that can last for years. Thousands of people die in wars. Buildings, bridges, forests, and homes are destroyed. Animals are killed too. Families are separated.

People often ignore wars in other countries because their own homeland is at peace. Dr. King discouraged that kind of thinking. He wanted people to be concerned about other nations. In his acceptance speech for the Nobel Peace Prize, Dr. King explained that war did more harm than good. He believed the millions of dollars spent on war could be used to help fight poverty, hunger, and other problems.

The Vietnam War was a civil war in the country of Vietnam. It began in 1954 and quickly grew to involve six other countries. The United States entered the war to help its ally, South Vietnam. Dr. King protested the Vietnam War because he believed the US government should have chosen peacemaking over fighting and should have used the money it spent on the war to help the nation's poor. He held anti-war marches. He talked about the harm war caused. And he encouraged ending war forever.

Dr. King's view about war was not popular. People felt he was not being patriotic. Dr. King acknowledged their opinions, but he remained convinced that war created more problems than it solved. Yet, realizing that a war-free world is a big dream, he encouraged hope for "a brighter tomorrow" in the face of war.

Isaiah 11:6 paints a picture of a brighter future too. Isaiah, a prophet of Israel, shared God's message about the kingdom of Jesus Christ. Isaiah envisioned a time when even predators would cease to harm their natural prey. Only God can bring about a world where lions don't attack lambs.

Today, there are wars scattered around the world. You may feel powerless to help, but remember the hope of Dr. King and Isaiah. Pray for peace. Pray for lives to be spared. And pray about how to help make tomorrow a brighter day, a day without violence.

It's true that nothing compares to the harshness of war. But life can be filled with so much conflict that it seems as if you're battling family, friends, or classmates. The only way to end fighting is to follow a different path than those who fight back. Be a peacemaker—every day.

Hope, pray, and act for a brighter future.

*Lord, please bring Your peace into
my life and into the world.*

21 DELAYED HOPE

 It is sad when you don't get what you hoped for. But when wishes come true, it's like eating fruit from the tree of life.
—PROVERBS 13:12

 A riot is the language of the unheard.

HAVE YOU EVER FELT ANGRY after being treated unfairly? Have you ever felt like no one could see you? Have you ever let anger out through yelling, stomping your feet, or throwing things? There's a kind of anger that bubbles up when people's hopes are crushed again and again. This kind of anger is seen in a riot, when a group of people destroy property and hurt others in a public place.

The United States had witnessed two recent riots at the time Dr. King decided to talk about them. One riot in Harlem, New York, occurred after police killed a fifteen-year-old boy. Rioters threw bricks to smash store windows and steal merchandise. Stores were boarded up, and some businesses had to close permanently. The other riot took place in Watts, California, after a bad encounter between a White police officer and a Black man. Over the next few days, angry residents set cars and buildings on fire. They kept firefighters from entering the neighborhood to put the fires out.

The people who rioted were angry about being trapped in neighborhoods with landlords who didn't care about heat, clean water, or reliable electricity. They were angry about being bothered by police when they were driving or just walking down the street. They were angry about what felt like two systems of law: a violent one for Black people and a more merciful one for White people.

This kind of helplessness and rage is at the heart of a riot, which is a group response to heartbreak. Dr. King attempted to explain that riots are not random acts. They are a reaction to hopelessness. He said, "As long as America postpones justice, we stand in the position of having these recurrences of violence and riots over and over again."

Enslavement, biased policing, and segregation choked out Black people's talents and dreams for hundreds of years. The poverty, lack of education, and limited choices were difficult to escape. Then their hopes rose with court decisions for integration such as *Brown v. Board of Education* and new laws like the Civil Rights Act of 1964 and the Voting Rights Act of 1965. But state and local governments were slow to accept these changes. Some Black people responded in destructive anger at broken promises.

When you see people acting in anger, find out why they are mad. What promises and hopes have they seen destroyed? You may not be able to make their situation better, but you can give them hope by keeping a promise of kindness.

Stand up for peace by paying attention to those who hurt.

Holy Spirit, help me see the broken promises behind anger and show me how to help.

22 A STONE OF HOPE

"I tell you the truth. You can say to this mountain, 'Go, mountain, fall into the sea.' And if you have no doubts in your mind and believe that the thing you say will happen, then God will do it for you."

—MARK 11:23

With this faith we will be able to hew out of the mountain of despair a stone of hope.

DR. KING IS A HERO to many people. But he didn't have superpowers. His strength came from faith! Faith in God helped him get through tough days. It made him believe in hope even when facing a mountain of struggles. Faith can help you too.

Dr. King learned about faith as a child. He was a preacher's kid, and he heard many sermons growing up. He learned that faith in God keeps hope alive. When he became a preacher and speaker himself, he often spoke about faith and hope.

Dr. King faced struggles just like everyone does. But he believed that life could get better! Today, Dr. King's messages of hope can be seen at the Martin Luther King Jr. Memorial in Washington, DC, which honors his life and accomplishments with sculptures.

The memorial includes many of Dr. King's quotes carved into stone. One quote carved into a portion of Dr. King's sculpture describes a "stone of hope." These words are from Dr. King's famous "I Have a Dream" speech. He gave the speech not far from where the memorial is today.

The memorial also has an area with a stone mountain called the Mountain of Despair. The Stone of Hope stands in front and looks like it has been cut from the middle of the mountain. This thirty-foot sculpture shows Dr. King emerging from the rock. It represents hope's power to break through despair. Sculptor Lei Yixin crafted the sculpture based on hundreds of pictures of Dr. King.

Jesus said that great faith is like having the power to move mountains. Are there mountains of difficult times, fears, or sadness in your life? Focus on something that helps you trust God in the middle of it. Remember a time that God helped you in the past. Learn some

names used for God in the Bible, such as *Jehovah-Jireh*—the Lord Will Provide—and *Jehovah-Raah*—the Lord My Shepherd. Or make a poster based on today's Bible verse or quote. No matter how bad things are in your life, remember to hope in God. He is able to bring good out of bad.

Look for hope in hard places.

Lord, help me be a stone of hope for my friends and family.

23 A CHANGE OF HEART

Because of Christ we now have peace. Christ made both Jews and non-Jews one people. They were separated as if there were a wall between them. But Christ broke down that wall of hate by giving his own body.
—EPHESIANS 2:14

Love is the only force capable of transforming an enemy into a friend.

UNDER THE DARK SKY of an early December morning, Dr. King boarded a bus in Montgomery, Alabama, and took a window seat near the front. His friend, a White pastor from Texas, sat next to him. This day was a long time coming. Dr. King and a few other civil rights leaders were riding an integrated bus for the first time!

The Black citizens of Montgomery had been boycotting the buses because of segregation. They stayed off the buses for over a year until they were allowed to ride alongside White passengers.

Finally, the Supreme Court decided that segregated buses were illegal—and not just in Montgomery, but all over the country. The boycott worked! Dr. King and his friends rode on the first bus that morning in victory. The invisible wall that kept Black people in the back of the bus was destroyed. But laws were one thing; people's hearts were another.

At a gathering to celebrate, Dr. King cheered alongside the people. But he also warned that the return to the buses would not be easy. Many White people were unhappy about the change. They might try to hurt Black people or speak rudely to them as they tried to sit anywhere on the buses. But Dr. King hoped that would not be the only possible outcome. He urged Black people to respond with dignity, self-control, and love. He said, "We seek an integration based on mutual respect. . . . We must now move from protest to reconciliation."

Reconciliation means making up with someone and healing a broken relationship. Dr. King wanted Black people and White people to make room for the possibility of friendly chat and kindness on the newly integrated buses. He asked people to make room for a change of heart.

It takes bravery to open your heart after being hurt. It is a truly otherworldly act. God's love is also otherworldly. The love you can show with God's power is unlimited. It can turn an enemy into a friend. Do you have any enemies? Open your heart to the idea of being friends with them. Ask God to help you love them.

Respond to enemies with self-control and love.

Holy Spirit, soften hearts as I show love to those who hurt me.

24 DECIDE TO LOVE

Love is not rude, is not selfish, and does not become angry easily. Love does not remember wrongs done against it.
—1 CORINTHIANS 13:5

I have decided to love. . . . If you are seeking the highest good, I think you can find it through love.

DR. KING LOVED THE PEOPLE who bombed his house.

Yes, you read that correctly. Dr. King *loved* the people who terrified his family and forced them to run into the night to escape the flames.

Who do you really, really dislike? Can you imagine *loving* that person? Even the thought can be challenging. For Dr. King, though, loving the people who harmed him did two things: First, love marked him as a follower of Jesus. Second, love kept him hopeful for the future.

Dr. King took many opportunities to talk about the connection between love and nonviolent resistance. He preached and spoke often to help people understand Jesus Christ's teaching on loving enemies. He believed that love is the best strategy to counter racism and violence.

In one sermon, Dr. King shared about three different types of love. First, he explained about love that is romantic versus love that is between friends. Then he talked about *agape* love. This love "is the love of God operating in the human heart," Dr. King told listeners. God's *agape* love is powerful because it invites violent people to stop and change. *Agape* love invites people to respond to goodness. This love creates hope for change and hope for the future.

Dr. King admitted that it was impossible to *like* the people who bombed his house. But he chose to love them because he received the power to love from Jesus.

What about you? Do you face someone who treats you with hate? If so, open your heart to God's love. Let it show you how to treat people with love, even those you don't like! You'll know you are succeeding when you help someone with a classroom assignment even though you don't like them. You will show *agape* love by speaking kindly to those who talk trash to you. And you'll know you're operating in God's love when you don't think twice when asked to work in the same group as someone who considers you an enemy.

Everyone has enemies. No matter how nice you act, someone will simply not like you. Or you may dislike a person so much that you think of them as your enemy. Just remember: God does not ask you to like them. He calls you to love them.

Show *agape* love to everyone.

*Lord, please help me love people
even when I don't like them.*

25 KEEP IT FRESH

 Can both fresh water and salt water flow from the same spring?
—JAMES 3:11 NIV

 Let us not seek to satisfy our thirst for freedom by drinking from the cup of bitterness and hatred.

YOU CAN FOCUS ON THE WOUND, or you can focus on the sneeze.

After being attacked, Dr. King chose to focus on a sneeze instead of his wound.

One day in 1958, Dr. King sat at a little desk in the lobby of a New York City department store. He was there as an author, surrounded by copies of his first book, *Stride Toward Freedom*. A long line of admirers waited to greet him. His fingers must have ached from signing so many copies! A woman asked him if he was Martin Luther King, and of course, he said he was. Suddenly, Izola Curry stabbed Dr. King. She was mentally ill and thought Dr. King was dangerous. Dr. King was rushed to Harlem Hospital, where they carefully took out the blade after hours of surgery.

Years later, Dr. King talked about how close the blade was to his heart: "If I had merely sneezed, I would have died." Dr. King had a choice: Would he focus on the painful wound and the person who hurt him, drinking a dose of bitterness each day? Or would he shift focus to the miracle of not sneezing and instead sip on refreshing gratitude?

Dr. King said, "If I had sneezed, I wouldn't have had a chance later that year, in August, to try to tell America about a dream that I had

had. If I had sneezed, I wouldn't have been down in Selma, Alabama, to see the great movement there. If I had sneezed, I wouldn't have been in Memphis to see a community rally around those brothers and sisters who are suffering." He could have let the attack, and folllowing assaults and threats, change his message to revenge and bitterness. But Dr. King decided to focus on God's gift of protection and the good that followed. For the rest of his life, Dr. King consistently spoke and acted with love.

The Bible teaches that our speech has power: it can build up or tear down. We can speak words that feel like fresh water to a person thirsty for encouragement and kindness. Or we can speak bitter words that seem like salt water, unfit to drink. People who follow God talk and react in ways that bring life.

Bad things will happen to us and to people we care about. This can be painful. But we always have a choice: Will we allow the bad things to fill our words and actions with bitterness and anger? Or will we pour out love and gratitude when times are difficult?

Focus on the blessings instead of the problems.

Holy Spirit, please bring justice to people around the world who have been mistreated.

26 NO PAYBACKS

Do not do wrong to a person to pay him back for doing wrong to you. Or do not insult someone to pay him back for insulting you. But ask God to bless that person. Do this, because you yourselves were called to receive a blessing.
—1 PETER 3:9

He who works against community is working against the whole of creation. . . . I can only close the gap in broken community by meeting hate with love.

DR. KING ONCE WROTE ABOUT some of the horrible things that happened to him. "I have known very few quiet days in the last few years. I have been arrested five times and put in Alabama jails. My home has been bombed twice. A day seldom passes that my family and I are not the recipients of threats of death. I have been the victim of a near-fatal stabbing."

It would have been perfectly natural for Dr. King to want revenge. But he refused to bring about justice for himself by hurting others. Returning pain for pain did not belong in the Beloved Community that he so wanted to create. Dr. King was willing to absorb the pain of suffering to preserve the hope of community for the future. Dr. King believed in God's justice. He believed that God was in charge of his well-being as well as his enemy's.

Leviticus, a law book of the Old Testament, says, "A broken bone must be paid for a broken bone, an eye for an eye and a tooth for a tooth" (Leviticus 24:20). People were expected to pay for the damage they caused. The law was designed to make people think twice before becoming violent with others. Jesus fulfilled this law by paying His own life for our wrongs.

When Jesus taught, He shocked people by being more concerned with reconciliation than punishment for wrongdoers. Jesus called His followers to a higher law of forgiveness. As Christians we have been forgiven, so we should forgive instead of seeking revenge.

Christians often say, "God fights my battles." That doesn't mean that God always harms our enemies. But He does always bring justice. He may make sure people are arrested for doing wrong. He may make people pay you back if they mess up your stuff. Sometimes God even changes people's hearts. He makes them see what they've done wrong. He encourages them to change. They may even apologize to you or find other ways to make a situation right.

Don't do wrong to get back at people. Don't become a bully because you've been bullied. Bring light, not revenge. Dr. King once said, "The time is always right to do right."

Do what's right—even when wronged.

God, give me the courage and self-control to do right when wronged.

JOHN LEWIS

**February 21, 1940–
July 17, 2020**

J ohn Lewis stared into the distance at the waiting state troopers. Pistols hung from the officers' hips. Tear gas wands and clubs stood ready in their fists. John was leading six hundred freedom fighters across the Edmund Pettus Bridge in Selma, Alabama. They were marching for voting rights.

John had become a civil rights leader while attending college in Nashville, Tennessee. His first arrest was for sitting in at a lunch counter in Nashville. As a college student, John became the chairman of the Student Nonviolent Coordinating Committee (SNCC) and a friend of Martin Luther King Jr. When he returned home to Alabama, he continued protesting unfair laws.

The plan that day in Selma was to march more than fifty miles from Selma to the state capital of Montgomery. The march had just started on March 7, 1965, when the troopers stopped the protesters and ordered them to turn around. Instead, John led the group forward, and the troopers attacked. They beat marchers and released tear gas. A trooper struck John and fractured his skull. Three other marchers died. When the news stations aired the scenes all over America, they called it "Bloody Sunday."

As images of the violence marred TV screens and newspaper pages, outrage rose across the nation. Voting rights for Black people became a top priority in Congress, and the Voting Rights Act became law that same year.

John Lewis continued his fight for voting rights and justice as a member of Congress for thirty-five years. He viewed the struggle for justice as a lifetime goal. "Freedom is the continuous action we all must take," he wrote in his memoir. "And each generation must do its part."

27 AN ATTITUDE OF FORGIVENESS

Then Jesus said, "Father, forgive them, for they do not know what they do."
—LUKE 23:34 NKJV

Forgiveness is not an occasional act; it is a permanent attitude.

"SEGREGATION NOW, SEGREGATION TOMORROW, SEGREGATION FOREVER!" Governor George Wallace yelled into a microphone. The governor was determined to maintain racism as long as he was in charge in Alabama. Governor Wallace was a terror to Black people and to any supporters of the civil rights movement, and he enjoyed it. He gave racists permission to be violent. Alabama police officers beat and trampled Black people with horses. Klan members burned crosses on the lawns of Black people's homes. Wallace sent state troopers to gas and beat peaceful marchers in Selma, Alabama—the awful event called Bloody Sunday. Wallace fought with all his power as governor to keep justice from Black people.

Years later, George Wallace was shot several times. He lived, but he was paralyzed. Shirley Chisolm, the first Black woman to run for president, went to the hospital to check on him. Her undeserved kindness broke something in him. George began to publicly apologize for the violence he caused. "I did stand, with a majority of White people, for the separation of the schools," he said. "But that was wrong, and that will never come back again."

Some people ignored Wallace's apologies. He had caused so much pain. But John Lewis, a victim of Bloody Sunday, listened. "Through genuine repentance and forgiveness, the soul of our nation is redeemed," John wrote. When George Wallace ran for governor of Alabama again in 1982, Black voters elected him. It was forgiveness at the ballot box, which he had once kept from them.

It's not easy to ask for forgiveness or offer forgiveness. But it is the way of Jesus. Jesus even asks His followers to wait to worship God in order to first ask forgiveness of someone we have wronged (Matthew 5:23–24).

Loving God requires a willingness to follow God's example. God forgives our sins. He forgives our mistakes. And He forgives us over and over and over again. Jesus even asked the Father to forgive the soldiers who nailed Him to the cross (Luke 23:34).

Forgiveness is both heard and seen. Dr. King called forgiveness "a permanent attitude," a way of life. Only God can help you forgive forever like that! Dr. King was a man of God. He had the Spirit of God to help him forgive so completely. If you are a follower of God, the Spirit of God will help you too.

Have an attitude of forgiveness like Jesus.

Holy Spirit, help me have a heart ready to forgive and to ask for forgiveness.

28 HOW TO WIN A FRIEND

 "Blessed are the peacemakers, for they will be called children of God."
—MATTHEW 5:9 NIV

 Nonviolence seeks not to humiliate and not to defeat the oppressor, but it seeks to win his friendship and his understanding.

WHEN DARYL DAVIS WAS TEN years old, he was bullied by a group of White people. (Daryl is Black.) They threw rocks and bottles at him. He could not understand why they would treat him so terribly without even knowing him.

This question—"How can you hate me when you don't know me?"—stayed with Daryl as he grew. He became a musician and sometimes played in places where white supremacists hung out. One day, Daryl talked to one of them. The man shared a lot of stereotypes about Black people. Daryl just listened patiently at first, then asked questions. The man began to doubt the things he believed. Something about the way Daryl listened to him made him think about whether what he believed was true. Over the next twenty years, that man, and at least two hundred other white supremacists, walked away from racism and into friendship with Daryl. He has a collection of KKK robes his friends have given him after they left the hate group.

Daryl Davis shares a belief with Dr. King in keeping the door open for oppressors to walk into the light of love. Dr. King believed enemies could be reconciled—reconnected in forgiveness—with the people they once hurt. This idea is at the heart of nonviolent resistance: to call attention to the systems that are bad without humiliating or condemning the wrongdoers.

It is very hard work to hope in change and reconciliation when you have been hurt. It takes patience and tenderness. It takes strength that only God can give in order to remain open and loving toward an oppressor. No wonder Jesus called peacemakers "blessed." To be reconciled is a beautiful miracle.

Make peace with someone today.

Lord, help me not fear rejection as I reach out to people to make peace.

29 A COMMUNITY OF LOVE

Defend the orphans and the weak. Defend the rights of the poor and suffering.
—PSALM 82:3

I have the audacity to believe that peoples everywhere can have three meals a day for their bodies, education and culture for their minds, and dignity, equality and freedom for their spirits.

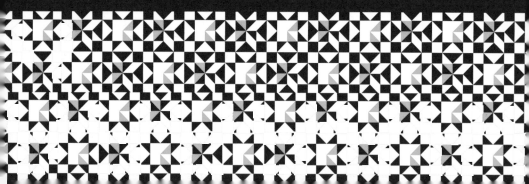

RICH OR POOR, BLACK OR WHITE, everyone gets hungry. Sadly, everyone doesn't have the same access to money or food. In 1967, there was a lot of hunger in America. In the South, nearly half of people were considered poor. Additionally, Black people were twice as likely not to find a job as White people. Hunger affected Americans of every background. Dr. King wanted to do something about it.

He gathered with other leaders of the Southern Christian Leadership Conference (SCLC). On the agenda was how to get the government to hear the voices of poor people of all races and cultures—Jews, Mexicans, Puerto Ricans, Black people, and White people—crying out for jobs and housing. The leaders landed on a solution they called the Poor People's Campaign. They would march on Washington, DC, to get politicians' attention. They would build a Resurrection City of tents and shacks in front of government buildings.

"Our idea was to dramatize the whole economic problem of the poor," Dr. King wrote in his autobiography.

When the SCLC met in November 1967, the leaders planned the campaign as a series of nonviolent protests. The final event would be a march in Washington, DC, the next summer. Sadly, Dr. King was killed months before. But the march still happened. On June 19, 1968, thousands of people from across the country gathered in the nation's capital. Over three thousand people camped in Resurrection City for over a month. The Poor People's Campaign drew attention to the issue of poverty. Afterward, one thousand food programs were launched to fight hunger in the neediest parts of the country. Congress agreed to spend $243 million to feed hungry children in school lunch programs.

Dr. King spoke against poverty because it is good and righteous to protect the poor. Throughout the Bible, God tells His people to care for the vulnerable. Caring for poor people is evidence of a community that loves God.

Today one in ten families lives in poverty. Will you let God meet needs through you? Organize a food or clothing drive for people in need. Volunteer at a fundraiser. Bake desserts for an organization sponsoring holiday dinners. Use your chore money to buy a birthday present for a child who has lost a parent. Live out the Bible's words as you defend the poor and help the suffering.

Use your time and money to help people in need.

Lord, show me ways to help poor people.

30 YOU HAVE A CHOICE

Then the Lord told Moses, "Go to the king of Egypt. Tell him, 'This is what the Lord, the God of the Hebrews, says: Let my people go to worship me.'"
—EXODUS 9:1

Oppressed people cannot remain oppressed forever.

SOMETIMES, WE READ STORIES that seem so far from the way we live that it's hard to picture them. When you read in the Bible about Moses and the people of Israel enslaved in Egypt, do you feel the ache of your back after endless days gathering straw and making mud for bricks? Do you feel the dirt caking your fingers? Can you feel the cry in your own heart for God to rescue you? It takes that kind of connectedness to understand why people will risk everything for freedom.

In the same way, to understand the risks of civil rights activists, you must understand the terrible conditions Black people lived under. Dr. King described living in Alabama in his book, *Why We Can't Wait*:

> You would have found a general atmosphere of violence and brutality in Birmingham. Local racists intimidated, mobbed, and even killed Negroes. . . . From the year 1957 through January of 1963, . . . seventeen unsolved bombings of Negro churches and homes of civil rights leaders occurred.

The civil rights movement was needed because of the unfair treatment of Black people. People still need to get involved because problems still exist. The good news is that things have gotten better in many ways. The progress came because brave people stood up to racist systems, just as Moses stood up to Pharaoh.

Dr. King's work as a civil rights leader was based on the belief that things would get better. His faith in God gave him hope. Dr. King believed the Bible stories about people being oppressed and how God set them free. He was confident that God would help Black people too. God's faithfulness in the past helped Dr. King see a future that did not yet exist.

You have a choice. You can pay attention to oppressed people and stand with them, like Moses and Dr. King. Or you can ignore the pain of oppression like Pharaoh and many White people of Alabama. But understand that God promises freedom for His people. To be on God's side is to stand with the oppressed for a future of freedom. Can you see it?

Befriend a kid experiencing homelessness or who has just moved from another country.

Lord, if someone is hurting and I can help, please show me how.

31 STRENGTH TO LOVE

Then Jesus said, "Which one of these three men do you think was a neighbor to the man who was attacked by the robbers?" The teacher of the law answered, "The one who helped him." Jesus said to him, "Then go and do the same thing he did!"
—LUKE 10:36-37

The first question which the priest and the Levite asked was: "If I stop to help this man, what will happen to me?" But . . . the good Samaritan reversed the question: "If I do not stop to help this man, what will happen to him?"

JAMES ZWERG'S MOTHER PLEADED WITH HIM, "Don't go. Don't go. You can't do this to your father."

James had prayed and read the Bible after talking with his friend about joining the Freedom Riders—Black and White people who rode together on buses through the South when it was still illegal to do so. The twenty-one-year-old White man felt compelled to join because he knew that segregated transportation was wrong. But his parents feared for his safety. James's parents rejected him for putting himself in harm's way. Even without the support of his parents, James found the strength to get on the bus as an act of love and justice for his Black neighbors.

Dr. King knew about this special kind of strength: he called it the "strength to love." The strength to love is the ability to have a tough mind and a tender heart. A tough mind is able to observe something—news, books, places, conversations, shows—and figure out what is true and what is false. A tender heart shows compassion by doing something about bad situations.

One day Jesus told a parable of a good Samaritan. A man was lying at the side of the road, hurt and in need of help. Three people saw him on the road. A priest and a Levite passed by. But a Samaritan man, a people the Jews hated, used both his tough mind and his tender heart. He treated the traveler's wounds, gave him a ride on his donkey, paid for his stay at an inn, and arranged for the innkeeper to care for the man.

Dr. King wanted to encourage people to build up the same strength to love as the Samaritan in Jesus' story. He wanted White people to see their Black neighbors oppressed by injustice, care about making it right, and be moved to act. James Zwerg embodied this so well. He was yelled at and beaten badly for caring for his Black neighbors—but his actions helped end segregation.

Just like physical strength, our strength to love is built up when we exercise it. Good neighbors build up the strength to love by seeing, caring, and being moved to act.

Build your strength to love by practicing acts of kindness.

Jesus, guide me to be a person who sees, cares, and acts.

CHARLES BONNER

April 7, 1946–

Young Charles Bonner didn't understand the rules of life in Alabama. "I couldn't understand why the White kids had better school buses, they had better books than we did. . . . We went to a little one-room school with a potbelly stove in the back of my church." Why were Black people treated this way?

Then when he was sixteen years old, Charles met someone who gave him the tools to fight for change. Charles and a friend had car trouble in Selma. As they struggled to push the car, a man in a yellow button-down shirt and tie came to help. Bernard Lafayette was a leader in the Student Nonviolent Coordinating Committee (SNCC), and he invited them to join the group. Reverend Lafayette talked to everybody about registering to vote.

Charles knew that voting held the power to change. He wanted Black people in Alabama to have that power. He told his classmates about SNCC's voting drive. In less than a week, he gathered thirty-nine students to help. For the next two years of high school, he stayed involved. He marched. He talked to adults about registering to vote. He talked to other students about joining SNCC. Charles wanted to make sure every Black person of voting age had a voice in changing the present and future.

Charles started college at Selma University, but the school asked him to leave because of his freedom fighting. He moved to San Francisco, California, and graduated from law school. He has been a lawyer for over forty years. He still fights for civil rights through the law.

32 WORTH THE RISK

Greater love has no one than this: to lay down one's life for one's friends.
—JOHN 15:13 NIV

The true neighbor is the man who will risk his position, his prestige and even his life for the welfare of others.

BRUCE KLUNDER HAD A PASSION to live for God. When he was eighteen years old, he heard about the bus boycott in Montgomery, Alabama, and wanted to help. He raised funds and sent them to the boycotters.

After college, Bruce lived in Cleveland, Ohio, where he worked for a Christian organization. He wanted everyone to understand that southern Black people were in fear for their lives and see the importance of helping, so he took youth to the South to see segregation for themselves. But racism wasn't happening just in the South. Right in Ohio, schools and housing were segregated. Bruce regularly protested injustice in his home state.

In 1964, Bruce decided to protest at the building site of a new school that was going to be segregated. He lay down behind a bulldozer, while other protesters lay in front of it. Sadly, the bulldozer backed over him and killed him.

Was it worth the risk? What about Bruce's family—his young children? Would they understand why their father gave his life? Bruce's wife said, "I pray that by the time the children grow up, their father's death will have been redeemed, and they will be able to see the effect of what his dying did for the consciences of at least a few people."

Mrs. Klunder and her children must have missed Bruce so much. But Bruce's sacrifice was not a waste. He influenced other White Ohioans to get involved with freedom fighting. Segregation in Cleveland schools finally ended in 1979.

Compassion is caring for someone else's needs. Jesus wanted His followers to understand that caring for others is important to God. He modeled this as He healed, fed, and talked to people. He modeled this in the ultimate way with His death on the cross. To follow Jesus is to be willing to sacrifice our lives by advocating for others, no matter what it costs us: friends, time, money, or even more.

Dr. King preached, marched, organized, and suffered so that Black people could gain rights as citizens. He encouraged people to risk helping others too. He believed that compassionate people are involved people. They do not look from a distance when someone is hurting. That is what Jesus lived and died for. According to God, helping people is always worth the risk.

Be willing to give up what you want to help others.

Lord, help me have the courage to get involved and help others, no matter the risk.

33 SILENCE HURTS

Speak up for those who cannot speak for themselves.
Defend the rights of all those who have nothing.
—PROVERBS 31:8

In the end, we will remember not the words of our
enemies, but the silence of our friends.

MOST OF THE PHOTOS of Thurgood Marshall look pretty serious. He is usually gazing into the distance in a dark suit or black robe, eyebrows crinkled with intensity. But when Thurgood was a boy, he loved pranks. And his pranks actually led him to study law!

One day, young Thurgood pulled a prank and got caught by the school principal. His punishment was to read the Constitution of the United States. From then on, he was fascinated by and respected the law. He decided to be a lawyer.

Thurgood Marshall worked as a lawyer representing Black people in civil rights cases in court. Sometimes Black people were unfairly accused of committing crimes. Or they were arrested for breaking Jim Crow laws. For example, police would arrest Black people for breaking driving laws because they wanted to punish people who were not taking the bus during a boycott. Mr. Marshall represented the accused people in court as their defense lawyer. He was also an adviser to Dr. King during the Montgomery Bus Boycott, offering legal advice so that activists and boycotters could avoid being taken to court.

Thurgood Marshall is most famous for the Supreme Court case

Brown v. Board of Education. As the lawyer for Black families, he argued against laws that forced Black and White children to go to separate schools. The unequal schools meant Black children got a worse education. The court agreed. They ruled that segregated schools were not legal. This case changed education equality in America. Mr. Marshall became a federal judge, and then in 1967, he became the first Black Supreme Court justice. He served on the nation's highest court for twenty-four years.

Dr. King and Justice Marshall did not agree on civil disobedience. Dr. King believed in breaking unjust laws. Justice Marshall believed in fighting injustice through the legal system. Yet Justice Marshall still worked with Dr. King and defended people who practiced civil disobedience. He did not stay silent. And the leaders' different views did not stop them from working together.

Be a friend who fights for others. Use your voice—in speech, in writing, through art, or simply through your presence at a protest event. Defend people who have been wronged. Just don't be silent.

> ## Speak up to help those who need defending.
>
> *Holy Spirit, please help me find the right way to express the need for justice.*

34 POWER FOR CHANGE

Don't let anyone look down on you because you are young. Set an example for the believers in what you say and in how you live.
—1 TIMOTHY 4:12 NIrV

As a result of their disciplined, nonviolent, yet courageous struggle, they have been able to do wonders in the South, and in our nation.

YOUNG PEOPLE HAVE THE POWER to create change. Do you realize that the good things you enjoy today are partly possible because children and teens stood up for their rights in the past? Unlike young people in the 1950s, you can go to the movies with a friend who is not your same race. You can eat with anyone you wish at a favorite restaurant. And any child living close by is able to go to the neighborhood school. Yes, you are enjoying the benefits of past people's "disciplined, nonviolent, yet courageous struggle" for change.

Children of all ages were involved in the civil rights movement. Some were as young as five years old, but they were all old enough to set examples worth following. They joined marches in cities across the nation. They participated in protests. They attended planning meetings. They made signs. They sang in choirs. And they remembered to stay true to Dr. King's teachings about nonviolent resistance. These children impressed Dr. King. He celebrated that their actions helped change daily life for Black people in the United States.

Not every adult viewed children's participation the same way that Dr. King did. Many felt children should be quiet and obedient. Some felt children should stay out of grown folks' business. Others worried about children getting hurt. Some thought children were just too young to understand what they were doing. But many children chose to speak up about what they knew was right. They acted with the hope, peace, and love that they wanted to see in their futures. They wanted to be a light for God during dark times.

In the Bible, Timothy was a young man who was a pastor to other believers. His mentor, the apostle Paul, wrote 1 Timothy to encourage his young friend. Paul knew Christians would use Timothy's age as an excuse not to listen to him. He encouraged Timothy to be such a great example that age wouldn't be a distraction to the work God wanted Timothy to do.

God has given you gifts to help others. So, don't let anyone look down on you because you are young. Pray about getting involved at school, church, or in the community. Ask God to help you do a good job. Let Him know you want to be courageous and work hard.

With God's help, you can do wonders.

*God, help me be a good example
today and in the future.*

35 STAND UP FOR TRUTH

But the Lord said to me, ". . . You must go everywhere that I send you. You must say everything I tell you to say. Don't be afraid of anyone, because I am with you. I will protect you," says the Lord.
—JEREMIAH 1:7–8

It seemed as though I could hear the quiet assurance of an inner voice, saying, "Stand up for righteousness, stand up for truth. God will be at your side forever."

DR. KING HUNG UP THE PHONE with a clatter. His heart thundered in his chest. The caller had just threatened his life in an angry distorted voice. Dr. King had received death threats before. Usually, he was able to feel peaceful anyway. But this time was different. He was very, very tired from his work and the call upset him. He thought about quitting his activism and just living quietly with his family.

As the caller's words rang in his ears, Dr. King bent over his kitchen table and prayed. "I am afraid," he told God. "I have nothing left." Then he felt God's peace, and his heart slowed. He heard God telling him not to quit. He knew that God was at his side. In that moment, Dr. King felt empowered and energized. He was ready to keep up the fight.

Three days later someone bombed Dr. King's home. Still, Dr. King remained calm. When he later wrote about the night of the threatening call and his conversation with the Lord, he said, "My experience with God had given me a new strength and trust."

With God's power, Dr. King remained steady in the face of much hate and violence. There were other bombings: his brother's house, his friends' houses, churches where he spoke, a hotel where he was staying. Someone shot a bullet through his front window. His enemies also told lies about him and twisted the meaning of his messages. They said he did not love America. They said he hated White people. Through it all, Dr. King kept telling the truth about the evils of racism.

Standing up for the truth is often not popular or easy. But it's the right thing to do. When you tell the truth, you are following God's example. The Lord is the God of truth. And if you're not sure what is true, start with God's Word. Check out what the Bible says. Then

pray about it, research the topic, or ask an adult. Know what's true and stand up for it. And trust that God will be by your side no matter what happens.

Trust God and follow truth.

God, thank You for being at my side as I stand for truth.

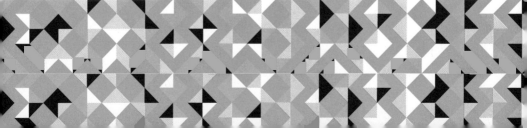

36 THE MOST POWERFUL WEAPON

So obey God. Stand up to the devil. He will run away from you.
—JAMES 4:7 NIrV

True nonviolent resistance is not unrealistic submission to evil power. It is rather a courageous confrontation of evil by the power of love.

THE BLACK CHURCH HAS BEEN a hub of faith and resistance for Black people since Africans were first brought to the United States. Sadly, the Black church was formed in part by White hatred—White Christians did not want Black Christians sharing their pews and worshiping beside them. So Black people formed their own churches.

When the government and society ignored Black people's needs, the Black church stepped in. Members worked together to provide for each other. Men and women had opportunities for leadership. Children were loved and valued. And churches became safe places to plan nonviolent resistance and get volunteers.

One Black church that was active in the civil rights movement was Bethel Baptist Church in Birmingham, Alabama. In the 1950s,

Fred Shuttlesworth was the pastor there. He and the members were dedicated to worshiping God through prayer, music, Bible reading, serving the community, and opposing injustice. The church raised bail money for arrested activists to get out of jail. It fed and housed freedom fighters. It was a center for protest planning. Reverend Shuttlesworth and his members also helped start a group of Christians across Birmingham that planned resistance to fight segregation. The people at the church protested for voting rights, school choice, and integration. The church was also a hub during the Freedom Rides of 1961, when Black and White people broke segregation laws and rode buses together through the South.

As a result, Bethel was a target for angry racists. Reverend Shuttlesworth received death threats. The church was bombed three times. Yet these evil actions did not stop them! The people of Bethel pressed on because they believed that God was on their side and in their work.

The Bible teaches us to not just avoid evil but to actively resist it. God's Word actually says to stand up to the devil! Dr. King believed that a key way to push back against evil was nonviolent resistance. He reminded people that we do not have to give in to evil. Love is the invisible weapon of nonviolent resistance.

Love is more powerful than evil. God can give you His power to resist hate and violence. God can also surround you with other people who are standing against evil. You don't have to do it alone!

Don't give in to evil. Fight it.

Lord, help me resist evil every day.

37 DON'T BE MOVED

You can have peace in me. In this world you will have trouble. But be brave! I have defeated the world!
—JOHN 16:33

Nonviolent resistance is not a method for cowards.

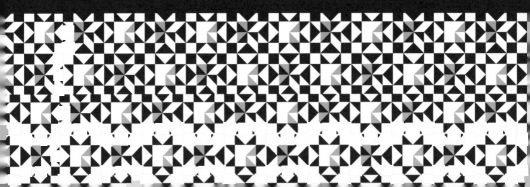

STICKY SODA DRIPPED DOWN the young men's faces. Slimy food slid down their clothes. Thick spit clung to their hair. The teenagers sat still like statues as they waited for someone to take their food order. No one did.

Sit-ins were nonviolent protests used during the civil right movement. Joseph McNeil and three of his college friends staged one of the first sit-ins at the lunch counter in Woolworth's department store in Greensboro, North Carolina. They were inspired by the nonviolent strategy that Dr. King used in the Montgomery Bus Boycott. They decided to resist the store's rule that said Black people could not eat at restaurants with White people.

On February 1, 1960, Joseph and his friends sat down. They asked for food. The server said no. They left but came back the next day with more friends. They sat at the counter until closing time, even when other customers poured food on them. No matter what people said or did to them, Joseph and his friends refused to fight back. The story spread in newspapers and on the radio. Hundreds of other young people showed up at the store to protest. Churches got involved. Business owners and other people did too. On July 25, 1960, Greensboro's Woolworth's finally allowed Black people to eat at its lunch counter. Other Woolworth's stores soon followed.

Sit-ins happened in other cities too. Many young people followed the example of Joseph McNeil and his friends. As the sit-ins and other kinds of protest spread, students took training in nonviolence. They learned to protest peacefully and not fight back. As Dr. King reminded people, nonviolent resistance isn't cowardly. It takes courage and strength.

Not everyone understands nonviolence, however. Other kids might call you weak if you don't pick fights or fight back. They might think you're a wimp when you try to solve problems with calm and peace. But remember that you don't need to be afraid because God promises to be with you. When you stand up—or sit down—for what's right without violence, you are being brave.

Don't be moved. Fight injustice with courage and calm.

Lord, help me stand up for what's right, no matter what.

MARILYN LUPER

September 17, 1947–

"**W**hat can we do now?" someone asked.

Marilyn shot her hand up high in the air during the NAACP Youth Council meeting. "Let's go downtown and sit down and stay there until we are able to drink a Coke," she said.

The students voted and the motion passed. Marilyn, at just ten years old, started the now-famous sit-in at Katz Drug Store in Oklahoma City in 1958.

Marilyn's mother, Clara Luper, helped lead the youth council for the National Association for the Advancement of Colored People (NAACP). Mrs. Luper taught them about nonviolent civil disobedience. She wrote a play about Martin Luther King Jr. Earlier in 1958, the members of the council had traveled to New York City to perform it.

Before that trip, Marilyn and the other children had never left the segregated state of Oklahoma before. When they arrived in New York, the children could use any restroom, eat in a restaurant, and try on clothes in the stores. Right alongside the White customers.

They returned home determined to make a change. Thirteen children, aged seven to fifteen, sat at the Katz's counter each day for three

days. White customers yelled at them and spit on them. Finally on the third day, they got their Coke. By the end of the year, Katz Drug Store ended segregated service at all thirty-eight store locations.

Marilyn and her friends were the first Black freedom fighters to sit in at a lunch counter anywhere in the country. Their example led the way for other activists to do the same.

38 START MOVING!

 Then the Lord said to Moses, "Why are you crying out to me? Command the people of Israel to start moving."
—EXODUS 14:15

 Courage is an inner resolution to go forward in spite of obstacles and frightening situations.

FANNIE LOU HAMER'S PLEADING FACE was captured on live TV. "Is this America?" she asked as she told her story. Because she had tried and tried to register to vote, she was fired from her job. Her husband and daughter were arrested and fired from their jobs. The police entered her home without a warrant. The water company charged her $9,000 even though she had no running water in her simple home. Miss Fannie Lou could not find work because no one would hire her.

Miss Fannie Lou was on television as a member of the Mississippi Freedom Democratic Party (MFDP). The MFDP members attended the Democratic National Convention of 1964 to try to convince the Democratic Party to seat them as the real representatives from Mississippi. The regular Democrats supported segregation, and Miss Fannie Lou and the other MFDP members wanted to be represented in Mississippi lawmaking.

When it was her turn to speak, Miss Fannie Lou talked about how she was beaten so badly in a Mississippi jail that she could not feel her arms—just because she wanted to vote. "Is this America? The land of the free and the home of the brave?" she asked.

President Lyndon Johnson held a press conference so the TV station would stop airing her live speech. But Miss Fannie Lou's words were so powerful that many stations aired her speech in the news time that evening—bringing her message to an even bigger audience.

Miss Fannie Lou won the sympathies of many of her listeners that day. Though she had suffered greatly, she kept moving toward justice. In all her actions, Miss Fannie Lou was known as a powerful voice and a calm presence. She sang spirituals to gather strength and encourage those fighting alongside her with the songs' messages of God's power and hope.

Like Miss Fannie Lou's story shows, Black people at this time were stuck behind a wall of injustice. In the Bible's book of Exodus, the people of Israel were also stuck. They had just escaped slavery in Egypt, but on their journey to freedom, they came to the vast waters of the Red Sea. With the army of Egypt chasing them and miles of water blocking their path, they were terrified. They cried out to God for help.

God answered, "Start moving!" And He parted the Red Sea to make a way forward for them.

Do you feel trapped and afraid? Does it seem impossible to keep moving? Pray for courage. Pray that God will give you wisdom to know where to step next.

Take a courageous step by tackling a hard task.

God, when I am afraid, help me remember to call on You. Keep me moving in the direction of righteousness.

39 GET UNCOMFORTABLE

Continue strong in the faith. Have courage, and be strong.
—1 CORINTHIANS 16:13

The ultimate measure of a man is not where he stands in moments of comfort and convenience, but where he stands at times of challenge and controversy.

AFTER SIX DAYS of being locked up for protesting for voting rights, Ruby Sales, Joyce Bailey, Richard Morrisroe, and Jonathan Daniels were released. They were a group you didn't see together in Alabama in the 1960s: two Black teenage girls and two White priests.

They each needed to find a way home, but first they were all thirsty. As they walked up to a store to buy soda, Jonathan and Richard walked in front of the girls. They expected harsh treatment from the store's White owner. Their fear was well founded.

Jonathan Daniels wasn't from Alabama. He was born in New Hampshire and was in school in Massachusetts to be a priest when he heard Dr. King speak. Dr. King called for more church leaders to join the fight for civil rights. Jonathan wanted to become an Episcopal priest to serve God and serve people, so he decided to leave his comfortable life and head south to support voting registration in Alabama.

As the group approached the store, a volunteer deputy stopped them. He aimed his rifle at Ruby Sales. Just before the shot went off, Jonathan moved in front of her. The blast was so powerful that both Jonathan and Richard were wounded. Jonathan died. The volunteer deputy was not arrested.

Dr. King talked about Jonathan: "One of the most heroic Christian deeds of which I have heard in my entire ministry was performed by Jonathan Daniels." Dr. King had also experienced the difficulty and danger of nonviolent resistance. He lived with the knowledge that any day he might be attacked—and sometimes he was. Dr. King and Jonathan Daniels both followed the example of Jesus, who chose the way of love and was mistreated and killed because of it.

Dr. King believed the true character of a person can be seen during uncomfortable times. When Jonathan faced hate, he proved to be selfless, brave, and caring.

Your character will be tested as you get involved in standing for right. Most of us will not face death, but we will experience rejection and discomfort when we fight for good.

Ask God for the power to remain faithful in uncomfortable situations. He will help you have courage and be strong as you stand up for someone being made fun of or stop a student from playing a prank on a teacher. Ask Him to help you show up as a strong, faithful supporter *every* day.

Get comfortable with being uncomfortable.

Holy Spirit, please strengthen me in uncomfortable situations.

40 SECRET WEAPON

 We fight with weapons that are different from those the world uses. Our weapons have power from God. These weapons can destroy the enemy's strong places.
—2 CORINTHIANS 10:4

 It is not enough to say, "We must not wage war." It is necessary to love peace and sacrifice for it.

SEPTIMA CLARK POINTED TO THE BOOK as she sat under the shade of a tree. "Again," she said to the bus driver. "Read it again."

The man sounded out the words slowly and carefully. Though he was a grown-up, he had never learned how to read. Miss Septima was about to change that.

The bus driver and many other students came to Miss Septima to learn to read in order to pass a test that was required for Black people to register to vote. The White voting officials made the test difficult because they did not want Black people to pass. Septima Clark made it her mission to prepare people to pass the test, as well as to sign checks and read contracts, bills, and tax papers. Doing these tasks for themselves would free Black people from having to depend on others to treat them fairly, which often didn't happen.

Miss Septima spent her life educating people. She was fired from her teaching job after forty years because she was a member of the NAACP. At sixty years old, she started a network of Citizenship Schools. In answer to the segregationists' war to hold onto power, she battled with the weapons of education and empowerment. Dr. King called Miss Septima the "Mother of the Movement" because her teaching equipped Black people to take hold of the freedoms they deserved. Miss Septima's Citizenship Schools gave Black people the tools to register to vote and the knowledge to use that vote wisely. Her teaching prepared young people to perform well in integrated schools. The books, newspapers, and other resources her students learned to read opened other worlds to them and connected them to a greater community of people who were demanding their rights. Miss Septima created a different kind of soldier—one who fought back with knowledge.

The Bible talks about the weapons of God. These are not weapons that cause physical harm, but tools that destroy lies and hate. Septima Clark's choice of weapon looked a lot like the ones Jesus used. Jesus used stories, Scripture, and knowledge to reach people, combined with self-sacrifice. He avoided any kind of violence.

Jesus' followers don't fight in the same ways as the world does. You can be a part of destroying opposition to God and to justice by sharing truths about God's love and people's value, helping others grow in knowledge of God and His Word, and spreading peace with kindness.

Be God's secret weapon.

Jesus, show me ways to fight for right by building people up.

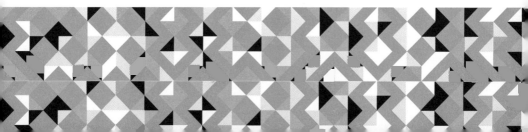

41 THE FLOW OF JUSTICE

But let justice roll on like a river, righteousness like a never-failing stream!
—AMOS 5:24 NIV

We are determined here in Montgomery to work and fight until justice runs down like water, and righteousness like a mighty stream.

WORDS RACED THROUGH DR. KING'S HEAD. He had just been made president of the Montgomery Improvement Association and was asked to give a speech. He had twenty minutes to think about what he would say.

Five thousand people had gathered after Rosa Parks was arrested for refusing to give a White person her bus seat. The people gathered that night had voted to stop using the buses in Montgomery, Alabama. They were tired of being treated as less valuable than White people. The people sang:

> *Onward Christian soldiers, marching as to war,*
> *With the cross of Jesus going on before!*

The song ended and it was Dr. King's time to speak.

Dr. King quoted from the Old Testament book of Amos. He said that as the number of boycotters grew, the people would be like water droplets pooling into a stream.

Drops of water can't stay still. They gather and run downhill, forming a stream. When a stream gathers enough water, it transforms into a mighty river that shapes dirt and rock. In a similar way, the civil rights movement gained power as more participants strengthened the flow toward justice.

The prophet Amos's call for justice to flow was a challenge to the people of Israel to return their hearts to God. Even though the people sang praises and made sacrifices to God, He was angry because they mistreated people as soon as the worship time was over. They claimed to be a nation of His people, but they did not protect the poor. They hated people who told the truth in courts. They couldn't stand people who spoke out against evil.

During the civil rights movement, many pastors and churches condemned protests and supported segregated worship. Organizations like the White Citizens' Council (WCC) and the Ku Klux Klan claimed to follow God, but they ignored the message of Amos. They terrorized people who stood up for fair laws and equal treatment. Dr. King repeated Amos's call for justice to flow.

How can you join the stream of people doing right? Always treat others fairly. Write letters to community and government leaders about issues you care about. Learn about the struggles immigrants, refugees, and others face. When you gather with people moving toward justice, a river of righteousness will wear down the dam of inequality.

Commit to showing fairness and kindness to others.

Father, help me show that I love You through how well I treat other people.

42 A VOTE IS A CHOICE

Then say to him, "The LORD, the God of the Hebrews, has sent me to say to you: Let my people go, so that they may worship me in the wilderness. But until now you have not listened."
—**EXODUS 7:16 NIV**

Give us the ballot, and we will no longer have to worry the federal government about our basic rights.

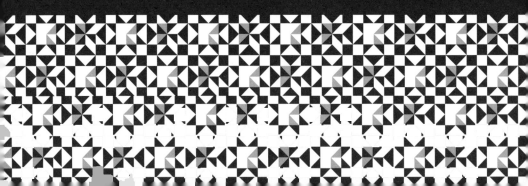

THE MORNING WAS MISTY. Men and women lined the street, wearing raincoats and hats or sheltering themselves under umbrellas. Yet their joy and excitement filled the street despite the gray weather.

It was Voter Registration Day in Selma, Alabama. There had been many other registration days in years past, but today was different. Today was the first time Black people could register to vote in Alabama in peace. No more poll taxes, requiring Black people to pay to do what was free for other citizens. No more reciting the entire Constitution by heart, or other challenging tests that were only asked of Black people. No more angry White officials and officers, bullying Black people as they tried to claim their rights as US citizens. Every face in the line beamed with dignity and pride.

For too long, White people at all levels of government had worked together to keep Black people from voting because they believed that Black people were beneath them. They believed that Black people having equal rights would be an insult to White citizens. They took these terrible beliefs everywhere: school, work, the voting polls, and even church.

Then President Lyndon Johnson signed the Voting Rights Act into law in August 1965. Dr. King was present at the signing. He witnessed the reward for all of the marching, resisting, going to jail, beatings, and lost jobs that Black men, women, and children had suffered. So many voices had cried out, "Let us vote!" Finally, the answer was a dignifying *Yes!*

In the book of Exodus, the Egyptians treated the Israelites as less. For over four hundred years, the Egyptians enslaved the Israelites. They robbed the Israelites of the basic human choices to decide their

work, family size, or where to live. The Egyptians treated the Israelites as if they had less value and dignity.

But God decided to set the Israelites free. They would have the ability to make their own choices, as He had intended. Because every person has value to God.

Dignity—the God-given worth and value of a person—is taken from people when they cannot act or worship or live for themselves. When a person is robbed of choices and forced to live beneath others, God is not honored.

Treat others with dignity. Offer honest compliments freely. Give a smile and try to be a friend when other kids are laughing in meanness. Don't join in when peers make fun of someone on social media. When you value others, you show them their real worth.

Offer people the dignity that God gives them.

Father, help me speak and act in ways that honor all people.

43 DON'T WAIT

"For I know the plans I have for you," declares the LORD, "plans to prosper you and not to harm you, plans to give you hope and a future."
—JEREMIAH 29:11 NIV

I have a dream that my four little children will one day live in a nation where they will not be judged by the color of their skin, but by the content of their character.

"GOOD CATCH!"

The little boy's smile spread at his father's praise. Then he launched the football back to his dad.

Dr. King had four children. Sometimes it was hard to be the sons and daughters of the civil rights leader. Other kids bullied them, and people looked at them with sideways glances. But at home, Dr. King was "Daddy." He played with his children, hugged them, and made sure they knew how valuable they were—though the world tried to make them feel unworthy.

Dr. King's children were one of the biggest reasons he fought discrimination with urgency. He wanted change *now*—for his little ones and all the other beautiful Black children growing up in a society that despised them.

Dr. King remembered how his six-year-old daughter and five-year-old son were so excited about an ad they saw on TV for an amusement park—Funtown! The rides! The fun food! Of course they wanted to go. But he had to tell his small children that Funtown was not open to Black children. And he had to watch his children's eyes cloud with angry tears.

Good parents want to offer their children safety, adventure, fun, and lots of love. Good parents want to help their children achieve their dreams. No parent wants to explain to a son or daughter that some people will treat them badly. No parent enjoys trying to explain a hateful system.

Dr. King wanted his children to have access to Funtown, but also to opportunities based on their skills and character. He wanted the best for them and was willing to do what it took to give them a "hope and a future."

God is a good parent too. In the Bible, the prophet Jeremiah told the people that they would be forced to live in another country among people who would not accept them. God told Jeremiah that this suffering would not last. His plan for His children was a good one, full of hope. God encouraged the people to make themselves at home. He told them not to wait for the native people to welcome them, but to make Babylon a place of peace for both them and their neighbors.

What do you hope for? Does it seem terribly far away? Ask God for His direction as you work toward your dream.

Pray for and work toward a better future.

Father, help me create the hope and future You want for myself, my friends, and all people.

ERNEST GREEN

September 22, 1941–

This was no ordinary first day of school.

Ernest Green climbed into one of the army station wagons. In front and behind this car were jeeps with machine gun mounts. Above them, military helicopters whooshed. Beside the jeeps, soldiers held rifles. Ernest and eight other Black students were being taken to school by a small army.

In 1957, Ernest was about to begin his senior year. He had volunteered to change schools to integrate Central High School in Little Rock, Arkansas. He expected little trouble because other city schools were integrated. But he was wrong.

Two days before Ernest's army escort, White people had attacked the Black students and stopped them from getting into the school. These people hated integration and wanted to stop it. After the attack, President Dwight Eisenhower sent the 101st Airborne Division of the

US Army. The soldiers had one mission: protect the Black students. With soldiers on each side, all nine students safely walked through the school's front door and into the 1957–58 school year.

In an interview, Ernest recalled, "It was then that I knew . . . we had finally cracked the door of segregation in Little Rock."

The students would later be known as the Little Rock Nine.

On May 27, 1958, Ernest became the first Black student to graduate from Central High School. His family attended the ceremony, and Dr. King attended as their guest.

44 PRAISE GOD

 The Lord gives me strength and makes me sing. He has saved me. He is my God, and I will praise him.
—EXODUS 15:2

 Free at last! Free at last! Thank God Almighty, we are free at last!

PRESIDENT LYNDON B. JOHNSON HANDED his pen to a grinning Dr. King. The president had just signed the Voting Rights Act of 1965. The law gave many southern Black people their first real chance to vote. The year before, President Johnson had signed another law—the Civil Rights Act—that made segregation and many discrimination practices illegal.

God used the civil rights movement to bring many blessings. After these new laws, community and civil rights groups across the country celebrated. *Praise the Lord!* echoed in churches from state to state. The words of an old spiritual, "Free at Last," rang out with new meaning.

Some of these mornings, bright and fair,
I thank God I'm free at last.

There was still work to do, but these laws offered Black people more access to rights than before. There were many reasons to sing!

They could sing about schools filled with children of all colors. The 1954 *Brown v. Board of Education* Supreme Court case outlawed school segregation, and the brave students including Ruby Bridges and the Little Rock Nine brought the law to life.

They could sing about integration in transportation. The Montgomery Bus Boycott of 1956 and the

Freedom Riders of 1961 had challenged segregated seating and won.

They could sing about the opportunity to eat delicious hamburgers, ice cream, and sodas at restaurants. The sit-ins of 1960 had forced businesses to open their doors to all people.

They could sing about the new laws protecting their rights. The Civil Rights Act of 1964 made it illegal to discriminate against anyone based on their race, religion, national origin, or color. It made sure public places were no longer segregated. The Voting Rights Act of 1965 outlawed the rules that southern states had used to keep Black people from voting.

Dr. King believed that God's power was at work during the struggles. God gave strength to the freedom fighters. God helped them march again after an arrest or beating. God provided them with creative solutions. And God sent helpers who were lawyers, teachers, and even presidents. That's why Dr. King could say, "Thank God Almighty!"

Thank God after every success, no matter

how big or small. Look for the ways He's working as you help make a brighter, happier world. He is there with you, and He is acting. Praise Him!

Celebrate God's goodness, and praise Him often.

Father, thank You that I can work by Your side.

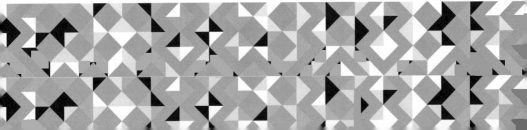

45 WHERE THERE IS JUSTICE

My friends, do not try to punish others when they wrong you. Wait for God to punish them with his anger. It is written: "I am the One who punishes; I will pay people back," says the Lord.
—ROMANS 12:19

True peace is not merely the absence of tension; it is the presence of justice.

"NO JUSTICE, NO PEACE!" Black protesters yelled as they marched toward a New York City police station in 1999. They were raising their voices against the killing of a Black immigrant, who was shot as he reached for his wallet to identify himself.

"No justice, no peace!" Black protesters yelled as they marched to protest the shooting death of another Black man in New York City in 2006.

"No justice, no peace!" Black protesters yelled as they marched in 2020 during the Black Lives Matter protests.

Each time, protesters called for the same thing: changes in the way police treat Black people.

Sometimes protests do not stay peaceful. The intention behind "no justice, no peace" transforms from a threat of disruption to a threat of destruction and violence. Some people yell the chant to say that they are willing to use violence as a form of punishment and to get what they want.

The Constitution gives you the right to protest. You can protest with a few people, or you can march with thousands. You can carry signs. You can yell sayings that express the change you want to see. You can engage in sit-ins and other resistance used during the civil rights movement. But stay peaceful.

Dr. King didn't believe justice could exist without peace. He thought that the world would be at peace when everyone was treated fairly. Justice is treating everyone the same. It means applying laws the same way to all people. No one is treated worse because of race, ability, or gender.

The Bible calls Jesus "the Prince of Peace" (Isaiah 9:6). You can trust the Prince of Peace to carry out justice. Have you ever wanted to take revenge on someone for treating you badly? Next time you feel that way, remember that God is just. He will punish evil in His own perfect way.

It is right to call out for justice. It is wrong to cause chaos and violence. It doesn't make sense to fight violence by being violent. Fight for civil rights. But don't try to gain justice by doing what is wrong. And always invite the Prince of Peace to go with you.

Keep peace in your home by refusing to pick fights or respond to those who do.

Lord, please help me trust You to bring justice.

46 ASK FOR MORE

When Jesus saw him lying there and learned that he had been in this condition for a long time, he asked him, "Do you want to get well?"
—JOHN 5:6 NIV

It all boils down to the fact that we must never allow ourselves to become satisfied with unattained goals.

ABLE TO GRAB A BURGER from the local diner? *Check*.

Able to drink from a clean water fountain? *Check*.

Able to go to a school of choice? *Check*.

Able to vote for people who have Black people's best interests at heart? *Check*.

By 1965, freedom fighters' marches, suffering, and blood had gained Black Americans the most basic of human rights: the right to live anywhere they liked, the right to attend good schools, and the right to vote. Dignity was being restored in the hearts of Black people. But these successes were just the start. Dr. King wanted Black people to know that they were loved by God and that God's love extended to their personal well-being. He wanted them to live as *full* citizens.

Dr. King and other civil rights leaders wanted racism and segregation to end completely. They wanted Black people to have access to good jobs. They wanted Black people elected to government. They wanted Black people to be free to purchase land and homes anywhere they desired. They wanted Black people to live without fear of harm.

By the mid-1960s, some critics thought that Black people should be satisfied and stop asking for more. Why did they have *so many* goals? Dr. King and other leaders ignored these questions. They knew that progress is not the same as equality.

In the Gospel of John, a sick man was lying beside a pool. The people believed that the first person to enter the pool after an angel stirred the water would be healed. But the man was never the first in when the water moved. One day Jesus came to that pool and asked the sick man, "Do you want to get well?" The man could only see his bad timing and lack of speed. Jesus offered a bigger vision—complete healing of body *and* soul.

The civil rights movement stretched Black people's imaginations. It helped them dream of a future when the country was not sick with racism, but healthy and whole. It helped them believe they could have more in life. More rights. More peace. More joy. More freedom every day.

What does your community need? Safer streets, a community center, a clean park? Setting a new goal and working toward more is an active way of asking the question "Do we want to be well?" Ask God for help in achieving your goal.

Want more? Make another goal.

List your hopes and dreams for your community.

Dear God, help me not be satisfied with incomplete justice.

47 IN STEP

They replied, "Let one of us sit at your right and the other at your left in your glory."
—MARK 10:37 NIV

And there is, deep down within all of us, an instinct. It's a kind of drum major instinct—a desire to be out front, a desire to lead the parade, a desire to be first.

THE DRUM MAJOR MARCHES to the center of the football field, bending her knees high with each step. She spins in circles, jumps high, and does a full split. She hops back up, marches again, then drops to her knees. Bending way back, her head touches the ground. Jumping up, she blows twice on a whistle and points her mace at the marching band. The musicians and dancers know the signal to begin the routine. The crowd cheers.

Marching bands are a fun part of Black culture. Some of the most famous marching bands are at Historically Black Colleges and Universities (HBCUs), which were created to educate Black students. Dr. King attended an HBCU named Morehouse College in Atlanta, Georgia.

Marching bands perform at football games, parades, and other events. Band musicians play loud, fast songs. Dancers kick, twirl, and move to the beat. Each band is a team. No musician or dancer is more important than another. But drum majors get lots of attention.

A drum major is a band leader. Some band students try out for the position only because they love being first. They want to be in control.

As Dr. King said, everyone has a desire to be first. There is nothing wrong with wanting a position out front. But he reminded people that being a leader is a big responsibility. Leaders can use their power for good or evil. Dr. King challenged leaders to do good by helping other people.

Only one person can be first. In the Bible, the disciples James and John thought they should be first. In Jesus' kingdom, they wanted to sit next to Jesus in positions of power. Jesus told them that God would decide who took those seats (Mark 10:40).

How does God choose leaders? God's leaders are humble. Jesus was the best leader because He cared about people instead of fame. He served people. He sacrificed for others. In God's parade, Jesus is the head drum major.

Good drum majors practice many hours. They don't act like they're the whole band. They thank others for their contributions. And sometimes they step aside and let a musician or dancer have the spotlight. If you're a leader, use your role to do good. If you're not, don't be jealous of others' success. Instead, look for ways to lead others to God's parade.

March to the beat of God's love by letting others be first.

Lord, help me keep in step with humility and love as I lead.

48 A CHANNEL OF THE GOSPEL

 Each one of us did the work God gave us to do.
—1 CORINTHIANS 3:5

 Keep Martin Luther King in the background and God in the foreground and everything will be all right. Remember you are a channel of the gospel and not the source.

SUN BEAMED INTO DR. KING'S CAR. He turned the dial on the car radio, and the notes of the opera *Lucia di Lammermoor* filled his car. It was one of Dr. King's favorite operas. Dr. King loved opera music because it tells a story.

His body relaxed as the singer's voice rose and fell. He felt peaceful driving through beautiful countryside on the sunny Saturday in January 1954.

He was headed to Montgomery, Alabama. Dexter Avenue Baptist Church had invited him to preach at its Sunday morning service. It was looking for a new minister, and Dr. King needed a job. He had other opportunities from a couple of churches to think about. A few colleges also had invited him to come teach. He was trying to discover which opportunity God wanted him to take.

That night he worked on his sermon. He wanted to impress the congregation. Should he include things that would prove how smart he was? Or should he just depend on God's inspiration as he usually did? As he considered the two choices, he reminded himself, "You are a channel of the gospel." He knew God would give him the right words. Dr. King prayed, then he went to sleep.

He got the job! God wanted him in Montgomery. The next year, Dr. King helped organize the successful boycott of Montgomery city buses. He quickly become a leader in the civil rights movement.

Many people consider Dr. King to be a hero, but he pointed people to God as the source of his leadership. He made God and the Bible the center of his messages.

If you become a leader, remember that you are doing God's work. You are His servant. Keep God first. Be yourself, but don't be a show-off. Jesus is the Light. Let Jesus shine through you.

Reflect Jesus' brilliance as you lead others to Him.

Holy Spirit, help me stay humble as I do God's work.

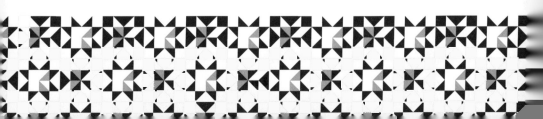

49 TRUE EDUCATION

Is there anyone among you who is truly wise and understanding? Then he should show his wisdom by living right. He should do good things without being proud. A wise person does not brag.
—JAMES 3:13

Intelligence plus character—that is the goal of true education.

DR. KING PAUSED AND LEANED IN to hear what the meeting attendees had to say. He focused on the words of every person who had feedback, praise, or criticism. There were many questions.

"Can we bring knives to defend ourselves?"

"What makes you think you can come over to Alabama to help us?"

"What is a pastor doing in protests and politics?"

The people at the meetings held many different beliefs and attitudes about Dr. King. Some didn't like his activism and thought he should stick to preaching. Others thought he was an educated snob who could not relate to poor Black southerners.

The people of Alabama were suspicious of Dr. King's plans for civil rights actions there. Dr. King had been a pastor in Montgomery but had left in 1960 to co-pastor with his father in Atlanta, Georgia.

Three years later, he returned to the state as a civil right leader. They resented how he had come back with a plan, but had not shared it. There were a lot of misunderstandings.

Dr. King held many meetings with local community, business, and Christian leaders. In his autobiography, he described the mood before one gathering: "The atmosphere when I entered was tense and chilly."

Dr. King listened well and weighed the worries of each speaker. He spoke to their fears and concerns. He assured them that there were no outsiders in the cause of justice. He gently challenged them that nonviolence meant no knives. He reminded them that the good news of Jesus wasn't just for heaven, but for earth, right now. By the time he finished, the mood had shifted. Many people even committed to getting involved.

Dr. King was an educated man. But having knowledge wasn't enough. People needed to know he was trustworthy. The way he listened and responded demonstrated his character, and he won the people's trust. Dr. King said that God gave him the power to change opposition into "faith and enthusiasm."

It's important to be educated. Learn all you can about the world's problems and possible solutions. But learn to listen and respond with love too. You will make the greatest difference when others trust you and are willing to work beside you. Be someone God can use by being someone people can trust.

Match your actions to your words.

God, help me be worthy of people's trust.

50 BE A STAR

So my dear brothers, stand strong. Do not let anything move you. Always give yourselves fully to the work of the Lord. You know that your work in the Lord is never wasted.
—1 CORINTHIANS 15:58

Be a bush if you can't be a tree. If you can't be a highway, just be a trail. If you can't be a sun, be a star. For it isn't by size that you win or fail. Be the best of whatever you are.

MISS GEORGIA SWIRLS THE CHEESES into the macaroni, then spins around to check the greens—they need a little more simmering time. She mops her forehead and smooths out her apron before she heads to the dining area.

"Tiny!" Dr. King greets Miss Georgia by a nickname. She smiles. She is not tiny. She is strong. In her house, she runs a restaurant. It is a safe and delicious meeting place for Dr. King and others to organize the Montgomery Bus Boycott.

When Georgia Gilmore heard that Rosa Parks had not given up her bus seat to a White woman, she was inspired. Right away, Miss Georgia joined the Montgomery Improvement Association (MIA)—the group that organized the boycott. When her boss at the cafeteria where she cooked found out that Miss Georgia was part of the boycott, he fired her on the spot. He probably thought he was hurting her, but this firing set her free to serve the movement.

Miss Georgia used what she had—her mouth-watering cooking skills and her no-nonsense attitude—and helped feed and support the people boycotting. She cooked for hungry boycotters. She collected donations from donors who didn't want to be known. She raised money through baking pies and cakes—enough to purchase cars for boycotters to carpool together!

She called her restaurant the Club from Nowhere. It was a place where Dr. King could go and not worry about the food or the company. The MIA was able to keep the boycott going for over a year in part because of Miss Georgia.

Miss Georgia used what she had in order to help other people. You can do the same. What do you love to do? What are your gifts? Can

you sing, or fold clothes, or mow lawns, or babysit, or cook, or code? Whatever your abilities, give them to God. God can take your gifts and multiply them to help people.

Offer your talents to God.

Father, use my talents and gifts to bless others.

CLAUDETTE COLVIN

September 5, 1939–

As Claudette Colvin paid her bus fare after school that day, stories of Black heroes filled her head. Her history class had discussed Harriet Tubman, Sojourner Truth, and Frederick Douglass. The teens also talked about the restrictions they were experiencing in Montgomery, Alabama, in 1955.

After she paid at the front door, Claudette left the bus, then entered at the back in the section for Black people. The bus quickly filled, and a White woman stood over Claudette. The law said that Claudette had to give up her seat for any White person who wanted it. Claudette had to stand. But Claudette did not move. The driver yelled at her, but still she sat.

Soon two White police officers stood over Claudette. "Get up!" one yelled.

Tears trickled down her cheeks, but she answered in a clear, high voice, "No, sir. It's my constitutional right to sit here as much as that lady. I paid my fare, it's my constitutional right!" As Claudette's school books clattered to the floor, the officers dragged her off the bus and into a police car. When the jail cell's lock thudded shut, panic washed over her. But then she prayed the Lord's Prayer and recited Psalm 23:1: "The Lord is my shepherd."

After Claudette's release, news spread. Some people thought the fifteen-year-old was a troublemaker. Others said she was brave. At her trial, Claudette was found guilty of violating the segregated bus law and placed on probation.

Nine months later, also in Montgomery, Rosa Parks refused to give up her bus seat. Rosa had been watching people like Claudette claim their rights. She had chosen to follow Claudette's example. Her refusal set off the Montgomery Bus Boycott, which eventually ended segregation on the city's buses. But Claudette had stayed in her seat first. She had helped get the people of Montgomery ready for Rosa.

51 TIME TO ACT

There is a right time for everything.
—ECCLESIASTES 3:1 TLB

Time is neutral; it can be used constructively or destructively.

BREE NEWSOME INCHED UP THE FLAGPOLE near the state capitol building in Charleston, South Carolina. She ignored the police officer shouting for her to stop. She grabbed the Confederate flag flapping from the pole. Many people, including Bree, believe the flag is a symbol of white supremacy. Bree brought the flag down. As her feet hit the ground, she was arrested.

People had been complaining about South Carolina's use of the Confederate flag for a long time, but the flag still flew—until Bree scaled the pole on June 27, 2015. The city permanently took the flag down weeks later.

Have you ever caught yourself thinking, *I'll do that later*? Maybe you wanted to run for class president to help create a new anti-bullying program. Perhaps you wanted to plan a rally or fundraiser to support a cause you care about. But you got distracted and went back to playing. Your heart said, *Go*, but your head said, *Not now*. And things did *not* get better!

During the 1950s and 1960s, Black people were denied the same rights as White people. Black people wanted to vote in elections. They wanted to live in any neighborhood they liked. As the civil rights movement gained strength, many people started to stand up against these injustices.

But Dr. King noticed that many people still put off action. These people were waiting—hoping and praying—for injustices to stop by themselves. They thought that with patience and time, the United States would become a more just nation for everyone. Dr. King disagreed. He called this idea the "myth of time." Dr. King warned that time is what we make it: we can use it to bring about something good—or not.

There *is* a right time for everything. Sometimes waiting and taking time to pray and plan is the best action. Bree and other activists planned how to take down the flag, and many of the protests of the civil rights movement were carefully planned for months. But the key is to be ready when God shows you the right time. Then get involved. If people don't help, things won't change. If things don't change, injustices will never go away. But you won't let that happen, right?

Use your time for making good things happen.

Lord, please help me act at the right time.

52 HEALING MESSAGES

Careless words stab like a sword. But wise words bring healing.
—PROVERBS 12:18

Nonviolence is a powerful and just weapon. Indeed, it is a weapon unique in history, which cuts without wounding and ennobles the man who wields it.

NINA SIMONE BELTED OUT THE WORDS at the piano as the band played guitars and drums around her.

You're young, gifted, and Black.
You got your soul intact, and that's a fact.

Her friend, writer Lorraine Hansberry, had encouraged a group of young Black writers that they were "young, gifted, and Black." The words had anchored in Nina's mind. The message was so needed, so positive, so powerful. Nina knew she had to make them into a song. She wrote for Black children, but the song became an anthem of joy and power for all Black people. It is still sung and recorded today.

During the civil rights movement, White people controlled the main news and media outlets. So Black writers and artists made their own spaces to tell stories and craft images that told a fuller story of

Black life. Black newspapers and magazines dedicated themselves to sharing honest stories about Black people's struggles. They also shared stories celebrating Black life that most papers ignored. They shared accomplishments of ordinary and famous Black people.

Writers, singers, poets, painters, and photographers used their media as nonviolent protest and to express Black joy, wonder, and determination. James Baldwin wrote an essay, "My Dungeon Shook," about the possibilities of an integrated America: "We can make America what America must become." Aretha Franklin sang an anthem of "Respect." Elizabeth Catlett carved a tall, dark-skinned woman reaching a strong fist toward the sky.

Dr. King preached fiery sermons. He shouted in protest about injustice during meetings. But he also spoke to middle school students about the possibilities in their futures. He described his vision of the Beloved Community, in which all people would live in peace and respect. In 1963, he spoke of the beauty and value of children at the funerals of the four little girls who died in the Sixteenth Street Baptist Church bombing. Love was his major theme. And love heals.

You too can use your words and creations to make the world better. Write stories and poems about beauty. Create art. Tell the world how you feel! But let your creations reflect your faith in Jesus. Let them shine God's light.

Create messages of hope and healing.

Holy Spirit, help me express myself in ways that heal.

53 ALL OF THEM

Pray in the Spirit at all times with all kinds of prayers, asking for everything you need. To do this you must always be ready and never give up. Always pray for all God's people.
—EPHESIANS 6:18 NCV

We want all of our rights, we want them here, and we want them now.

DR. KING HAD A FREE-FLOWING SPEAKING STYLE. He prepared his words, but he also went freestyle to share from his heart or address a current event. But this day in 1967, he read his prepared speech word for word. He wanted to say exactly what he had planned. He said that the Vietnam War was wrong and that the United States should exit the war.

> The world now demands a maturity of America that we may not be able to achieve. It demands that we admit that we have been wrong from the beginning of our adventure in Vietnam, that we have been detrimental to the life of the Vietnamese people. . . . We should take the initiative in bringing a halt to this tragic war.

The next day, President Johnson canceled King's invitation to the White House. Over 150 newspapers criticized him. They thought it wasn't his place to talk about international matters. They had lost respect for him. Polls showed that over half of Black people had also lost respect for him.

Dr. King felt alone, but he was sure that war was unjust.

Dr. King called poverty, racism, and war "triple evils." He could have easily focused on just one. Each evil was certainly big enough! But he felt that *all* these problems needed to be fought. Each of them harmed human beings. Fighting poverty *and* racism *and* war was fighting for civil rights.

Dr. King stuck to his purpose. Purpose is God's plan for a person's life. Dr. King began as a warrior against racism. But he didn't limit his or God's definition of civil rights. When he saw poverty across the nation, he organized the Poor People's Campaign. When he learned of suffering Vietnamese citizens and dying soldiers, he spoke against war. Wherever he witnessed evil, he spoke and acted against it—again and again.

Dr. King also prayed about these wrongs. He kept asking God for the same things: freedom for Black people; access to education, safe homes, and fair-paying jobs; and an end to violence around the world. He believed that God would eventually answer.

Do you know your purpose? Ask God to help you discover it. Ask Him for faith to believe beyond the limited choices that seem to be available. Then stick to the purpose God gives you as you keep trusting Him.

Expect God to do big things, and keep praying.

God, help me have faith to seek Your purpose for my life.

54 LOVE AT WORK

And whatever you do, do it with kindness and love.
—1 CORINTHIANS 16:14 TLB

Make a career of humanity. Commit yourself to the noble struggle for equal rights. You will make a better person of yourself, a greater nation of your country, and a finer world to live in.

MAHALIA JACKSON WAS A FAMOUS gospel singer who sang right before Dr. King's famous "I Have a Dream" speech at the March on Washington. Harry Belafonte was a Hollywood actor who donated bail money to jailed freedom fighters. Bill Hudson was a photographer whose newspaper images of protests and police brutality woke many people to the harsh world that Black southerners lived in.

Singers entertained at meetings. Lawyers helped people who were arrested. Writers shared the truth about injustice in newspapers, magazines, and books. Their work became an expression of their beliefs and their commitment to justice. People brought their unique skills and passions to the civil rights movement.

Dr. King's career was as a pastor. He was a teenager when he decided to spend his life serving God and people. He wanted to be a preacher like his father, Martin Luther King Sr. But his decision to be a pastor was not just about getting a job. He was dedicated to caring for people. He encouraged people to "make a career of humanity," no matter what kind of work they did. Making a career of humanity is not about the job you do. It's about your heart: how you treat people, and your awareness of the problems around you.

To make a career of humanity means being observant. What is happening with the people around you at school? At church? In your neighborhood? Who is in need of help or encouragement?

Sadly, there is always a group fighting for fair treatment. The world can be a difficult place to live in. Commit "to the noble struggle for equal rights." Your presence and your care for others makes you a better person and the world a better place to live.

God cares about your heart and your intentions. He can help you

help others right now, where you are, with what you have. Ask God: *Who can I help, and how?* Whatever you decide to do, do it with kindness and love.

Use your skills to serve others with love and kindness.

Lord, please help me find the ways I can best love others with my talents.

55 PURE MOTIVES

Do not be shaped by this world. Instead be changed within by a new way of thinking. Then you will be able to decide what God wants for you. And you will be able to know what is good and pleasing to God and what is perfect.
—ROMANS 12:2

The means we use must be as pure as the ends we seek.

IESHIA EVANS CAME TO THE PROTEST wearing a simple sundress. She had traveled all the way to Baton Rouge from New York City. She wanted to show her five-year-old son that she would do anything to make the world safer for him.

The July heat in Louisiana was sweltering, and so were the tempers of many people that day, July 9, 2016. Protesters were grieving and angry that a man had been killed by police officers. They blocked a highway so that drivers could not pass. Other people were impatient and frustrated by the interruption.

Police ordered the protesters to clear the highway, and many did. Ieshia did not move.

Ieshia wore a sundress that billowed with just a slight breeze.

The police wore helmets, bulletproof vests, safety goggles, and reinforced pants. They held batons, shields, and had holstered guns.

Ieshia stood sure, unarmed, her feet grounded. She would not stop her silent protest.

A pair of officers ran toward her and pulled her from the street. They took her to jail. A photo of the moment right before she was arrested shows the small woman, dressed for a picnic, waiting for the officers, uniformed for battle.

Ieshia's motives were pure: protest a man's death and set an example for her son. Her peaceful action highlighted the forceful approach of the police.

In the same way, Dr. King's nonviolent actions made clear the purity of his goals—justice and fairness—in the face of cruelty and hate. He and other protesters continued nonviolence even when assaulted with bombs at their homes and churches, burning crosses on their lawns, dog bites, beatings, and arrests. Dr. King's goal was not to scare others or to be vengeful. He did not bully like the racists did. His goal was justice. Dr. King knew that nonviolent action could show people their own brutality. With love, he invited them to change.

The way of many is to scare or force people into doing what they want. You don't have to look very far to find people who hurt others to get their way. But the way of Jesus is love. Jesus showed the purity of his goal by laying down his life. Jesus' goal was to bring people back to God.

Do you try to get your own way with siblings, parents, or friends? Ask God to change your heart and mind. Then you will be able to know and follow His good plans for you. Have the courage to be transformed by God's love.

Think about your motives and ask God to help you act toward others out of love.

Holy Spirit, let pure actions flow from a heart transformed by You.

56 FREEDOM'S RING

 The Lord is the Spirit. And where the Spirit of the Lord is, there is freedom.
—2 CORINTHIANS 3:17

 Let freedom ring.

PRESIDENT AND MRS. OBAMA TUGGED at a long rope. *Clang-clang, clang!* The 130-year-old bell rang out to announce the opening of the National Museum of African American History and Culture in Washington, DC, in 2016.

This bell is called the Freedom Bell. It is from one of the oldest African American churches in the country, First Baptist Church of Williamsburg, Virginia. "This bell represents the spirit of America," said the church's pastor. The bell was made in 1886, and for many years it rang to announce worship, weddings, funerals, and other events for the Black people who worshiped God together there.

Dr. King used the idea of a bell announcing freedom all over America during his "I Have a Dream" speech.

Let freedom ring from the prodigious hilltops of New Hampshire. Let freedom ring from the mighty mountains of New York. Let freedom ring from the heightening Alleghenies of Pennsylvania. Let freedom ring from the snowcapped Rockies of Colorado. Let freedom ring from the curvaceous slopes of California. But not only that, let freedom ring from Stone Mountain of Georgia. Let freedom ring from Lookout Mountain of Tennessee. Let freedom ring from every hill and molehill of Mississippi.

Dr. King not only studied the Bible, he followed the Spirit. He had a dream that America would remove the chains of racism that made us all prisoners of hate. His dream was to spread freedom to everyone. He rang out for freedom! You have that ability within you too.

The apostle Paul wrote that the Spirit of the Lord brings freedom. The Spirit came to announce that a new time had arrived: a time when the Spirit lives in people and guides them in a way He didn't during the events of the Old Testament.

We are like bells, in a way, when we ring in tune with the Spirit. We can ring out for freedom for our neighbors. We can sound an alert that all is not yet well. We can signal that this is the hour that change must come.

How does freedom ring within you? The way you follow the Spirit will look different than the way anyone else does because there is no one else like you. Think about how freedom can ring within you by asking these questions:

- What issue makes you angry?
- What do you think the world needs more of?
- What do you love to do?
- How do people describe your personality?

Ring to announce God's freedom.

Holy Spirit, guide me to ways I can announce Your freedom.

57 NO STOPPING POINT

God has chosen you and made you his holy people. He loves you. So always do these things: Show mercy to others; be kind, humble, gentle, and patient.
—COLOSSIANS 3:12

For when people get caught up with that which is right and they are willing to sacrifice for it, there is no stopping point short of victory.

DR. KING LET OUT A DEEP, ROLLING LAUGH. The friends behind him chuckled at the paper the officer had just handed him. The paper was a legal order stating that Dr. King was not allowed to hold a march he was planning in Memphis, Tennessee. The document meant that Dr. King and the other marchers could go to jail or face other punishment if they followed their plan for the march.

Most people wouldn't find a government order like that funny. But Dr. King had no plans to obey. He found humor in the effort to stop the march.

Dr. King was in Memphis leading protests against the working conditions of Black sanitation workers. After the deaths of two trash collectors, the other Black workers went on strike. The workers wanted more safety protections and better pay for the dirty job. They had stopped working almost two months before, but the city of Memphis refused to respond to their requests. Dr. King was planning the march to show the mayor that many people cared about the issue.

A few days before the march, on April 3, 1968, Dr. King gave a speech. He challenged listeners to show mercy to the sanitation workers who were on strike. He called for support and participation in the march. The 1,300 workers and their families were suffering without their paychecks. He urged people to join the workers in their sacrifice—even though that might mean going to jail. "I call upon you to be with us."

What cause are you willing to sacrifice for? Often, we sacrifice to meet goals we set for ourselves. We save money instead of spending it so we can pay for that thing we really want. We spend time practicing a sport or instrument so we can succeed at a skill. We study hard to

pass a class. But freedom fighters sacrifice for others. They put aside their interests to show mercy to people in need. Like the sacrifices of many people before you, your sacrifice can make the world better.

Sacrifice to make other people's lives better.

God, please help me sacrifice so other people can win in life.

58 FIT TO LIVE

Then I will go to the king, even though it is against the law. And if I die, I die.
—ESTHER 4:16

If a man hasn't discovered something that he will die for, he isn't fit to live.

DIANE NASH STARED AT THE official piece of paper. She paused to think about the heaviness of the moment. Then she folded up the paper, slid it into an envelope, and sealed it.

Diane was going to ride a bus with an integrated group through the segregated South in the Freedom Rides of 1961. Nothing would stop her. Not the Ku Klux Klan, who had thrown bombs into the buses of Freedom Riders before. Not the Birmingham police chief, Eugene "Bull" Connor, who refused to protect Freedom Riders from terrorists. Not even the federal government.

When the Attorney General, Robert F. Kennedy, sent his assistant to stop her from organizing and leading the Freedom Rides with John Lewis, Diane responded: "Sir, you should know, we all signed our last wills and testaments last night before [we] left [on the bus for Birmingham]. We know someone will be killed. But we cannot let violence overcome nonviolence."

What does it mean to be "fit to live"? To be fit to live is to know your purpose in life and to go after it with your everything. It's having the attitude of determination that Diane expressed before the

Freedom Rides. It's being so committed to living for something that you are also willing to sacrifice greatly for it.

This was true of Esther in the Bible. Esther did not have an easy life. Her people, the Israelites, were forced to leave their homes and live in another country. They had to hide the fact that they were Jewish in order to live. Esther's name was even changed from Hadassah in order to fit in. Esther was brought up by her cousin, Mordecai, because she was an orphan. And then she was taken from her cousin and her home again when King Xerxes chose her for his new queen.

Esther's cousin sent a message to her in the palace that a man in the government wanted to kill all the Jews. What would she do about it? Though Esther was afraid of King Xerxes, she decided that she would talk to him about her people. The king had the power to kill her for appearing in his court without permission. But Esther's mission was worth the risk. And her courage ended up saving her people.

Diane Nash and Esther were both brave and determined as they faced great risk. They did what others didn't want to do. Fighting for right can be risky. You might lose friends, opportunities, respect, or more. But you will not be the only one. Be the one willing to do more like Diane and Queen Esther.

> **Think about what you're willing to risk this week for kindness and right.**
>
> *God, show me how to be fully committed.*

DIANE NASH

May 15, 1938–

Diane Nash wanted to have fun! She had just moved to Nashville, Tennessee, for college, and she was ready to explore. She wanted to shop for cute clothes. She wanted to enjoy a hamburger with her friends at a restaurant. She wanted to watch a movie on the big theater screen. But she couldn't. Diane wasn't allowed in those places because of her skin color.

Diane was born in Chicago, Illinois, where Black people had more freedom. She was shocked by segregation when she arrived in Tennessee in 1959. She decided that she would not let discrimination control her without a fight. She joined a group of students opposing segregation through nonviolence.

In 1961, Diane helped found the Student Nonviolent Coordinating Committee (SNCC). This group trained students in nonviolence and organized protests. As a SNCC leader, Diane led voting registration campaigns, marches, and Freedom Rides. When riders were attacked, Diane refused to let the violence stop the rides. She sealed her last will and testament in an envelope in case of her death and boarded a bus.

Diane was at the center of the student movement in Nashville. She led sit-ins of lunch counters and a boycott of segregated stores. She sat in "Whites only" movie theaters. She led a march to City Hall. When the mayor came out, she boldly asked him, "Do you feel that [it's] wrong to discriminate against a person solely on the basis of his race or color?" Struck by her passion, the mayor admitted segregation was wrong! Nashville became the first city in the South to allow Black people to eat at lunch counters.

Diane didn't wait for others to lead. She believed that each person has a responsibility to act. Diane's fire, leadership, and direct actions inspired young people around the country to get involved and brought more rights to Black people.

59 SAY YES

Each of you received a spiritual gift. God has shown you his grace in giving you different gifts. And you are like servants who are responsible for using God's gifts. So be good servants and use your gifts to serve each other.
—1 PETER 4:10

I just want to do God's will.

HE DIDN'T KNOW IT, but Dr. King had only one day left to live.

In his final speech on April 3, 1968, he took time to reflect on his motivation for all the work, all the speeches, all the travel, all the protests. It all boiled down to this: "I just want to do God's will."

Dr. King also said in his speech, "I've been to the mountaintop." He used the mountaintop as a metaphor to explain that he could see change coming. He was so satisfied with this vision of change that he was no longer afraid of death. Dr. King's purpose was clear: he lived to serve God.

Dr. King focused on following God through the darkness of racism and discrimination. He trusted that as God's servant, he would always get direction from God. By reading the Bible, listening carefully to the wisdom of other peace-loving people, and praying, Dr. King had learned to listen for the instruction and direction of God. By faith, he said yes to following God's will.

How did Dr. King know about the changes that were ahead? He knew because he saw that God had already brought changes: the first

Black students to integrate White schools were graduating from high school; Black people and White people rode together on buses; many restaurants welcomed all diners to sit and eat; Black people walked out of booths with their votes counted. These changes were a result of the victories won by all activists: Jews and Gentiles, Protestants and Catholics, and Americans of every race and ethnicity.

Dr. King's obedience to God made the country a better place. Through him, God shone a light on segregation and inequality in the United States. It's hard to imagine what the world would be like today had Dr. King said no to doing God's will.

God has a plan for your life too. You won't always know the details, but you can learn to listen by studying the Bible, discussing it with trusted people, and praying. You can trust God's good plans for you. Say yes to being God's servant. Say yes to roles that help you grow as a young leader.

Listen for God's direction. Then follow.

Holy Spirit, show me how to be a humble servant of God.

60 FORWARD IN FAITH

Fight the good fight of faith, grabbing hold of the life that continues forever.
–1 TIMOTHY 6:12 NCV

The struggle to eliminate the evil of racial injustice constitutes one of the major struggles of our time.

MRS. CORETTA SCOTT KING WALKED AHEAD of the marching crowd. Under a black veil, her chin lifted as a tear gathered in her eye. She held hands with her seven-year-old son, Dexter. The two oldest King children marched alongside: Yolanda, age twelve, and Martin III, age ten. Only five-year-old Bernice stayed away.

Dr. King was supposed to lead the march. But now he was gone. He had been shot four days before, on April 4, 1968. He had died. Coretta brought their children to Memphis, and they marched in his place.

Many people in the country grieved Dr. King's death. Losing him was like losing the best of America. It was like losing Dr. King's dream. People were angry that a nonviolent person was shot. People were worried that with Dr. King gone, the dream of racial equality would die too. Mrs. King wished her husband was still alive. The children ached for their father.

Following his murder, Dr. King's friends worried about his family. They wanted Mrs. King and the children to be safe and comfortable. Coretta understood the worry, but she was convinced that she must continue to fight the evil of injustice. Her husband's memory would be best honored if the march in Memphis—and all his work—moved forward.

Mrs. King had already been an activist. She was involved in the fight for civil rights before she met her husband. During their marriage, she often sang and played the piano at charity events to raise money for the cause. After the Memphis march, she also stepped into Dr. King's leadership role by organizing the Poor People's Campaign. She went on to lead numerous anti-poverty actions.

Mrs. King founded the King Center to protect Dr. King's legacy and spread his messages of love, equality, and hope. Throughout her life, she spoke and wrote in defense of those who suffered. She worked to promote women's rights and participated in sit-ins to protest segregation in South Africa. She died in 2006.

Difficult times can make us want to give up. When you are tempted to give up because of hate or harm, look back and think of how far you have come. Remember the difference you have already made. Look at how your character and your faith have grown. Don't let circumstances tell you what to do. Let faith move you forward.

Allow your faith to push you through.

Holy Spirit, give me the faith to fight the good fight, no matter what hurt I experience.

SOURCES

Works by Martin Luther King Jr.

Books and Writings

Carson, Clayborne and others, ed. "Draft of Chapter XIV, 'The Mastery of Fear or Antidotes for Fear.'" *The Papers of Martin Luther King, Jr. Volume VI: Advocate of the Social Gospel, September 1948–March 1963*. The Martin Luther King, Jr. Research and Education Institute, Stanford University. https://kinginstitute.stanford.edu/king-papers/documents/draft-chapter-xiv-mastery-fear-or-antidotes-fear.

Carson, Clayborne, editor. *The Autobiography of Martin Luther King, Jr.* New York: Warner Books, 1988.

"Draft of Chapter III, 'On Being a Good Neighbor.'" July 1, 1962 to March 1, 1963, The Martin Luther King, Jr. Research and Education Institute, Stanford University. https://kinginstitute.stanford.edu/king-papers/documents/draft-chapter-iii-being -good-neighbor.

"Letter from Birmingham Jail." April 16, 1963, The Martin Luther King, Jr. Research and Education Institute, Stanford University. https://kinginstitute.stanford.edu/sites /mlk/files/letterfrombirmingham_wwcw_0.pdf.

The Measure of a Man. Chicago: Lushena Books. Originally published in 1959.

"My Trip to the Land of Gandhi." *Ebony*, July 1959, 84–92. https://kinginstitute.stanford.edu/king-papers/documents/my-trip-land-gandhi.

Strength to Love. Boston: Beacon Press, 2019. Originally published in 1977. Kindle Edition.

Stride Toward Freedom. Boston: Beacon Press, 2010. Kindle Edition.

The Trumpet of Conscience. Boston: Beacon Press, 2010. Originally published in 1967.

Washington, James M., ed. *A Testament of Hope: The Essential Writings and Speeches of Martin Luther King Jr.* New York: HarperCollins Publishers, 1986.

Where Do We Go from Here: Chaos or Community. Boston: Beacon Press, 2018. Originally published in 1967.

Why We Can't Wait. New York: Signet Classics, 2000.

Speeches and Sermons

"Acceptance Speech." December 10, 1964. NobelPrize.org. Nobel Prize Outreach AB 2023. https://www.nobelprize.org/prizes/peace/1964/king/acceptance-speech/.

"Beyond Vietnam—A Time to Break Silence." Speech on April 4, 1967, Riverside Church, New York City, *American Rhetoric*. https://www.americanrhetoric.com/speeches/mlkatimetobreaksilence.htm.

"Eulogy for the Victims of the 16th Street Baptist Church Bombing, 1963." MLK Visiting Professors and Scholars Program, Massachusetts Institute of Technology. https://mlkscholars.mit.edu/updates/2015/invoking-dr-king.

"Give Us the Ballot." Address Delivered at the Prayer Pilgrimage for Freedom, May 17, 1957, The Martin Luther King, Jr. Research and Education Institute, Stanford University. https://kinginstitute.stanford.edu/king-papers/documents/give-us-ballot-address-delivered-prayer-pilgrimage-freedom.

"I've Been to the Mountaintop." Speech on April 3, 1968, *The Martin Luther King, Jr. Encyclopedia*. The Martin Luther King, Jr. Research and Education Institute, Stanford University. https://kinginstitute.stanford.edu/encyclopedia/ive-been-mountaintop.

"The Man Who Was a Fool, Sermon Delivered at the Detroit Council of Churches' Noon Lenten Services." March 6, 1961, The Martin Luther King, Jr., Research and Education Institute) Stanford University. https://kinginstitute.stanford.edu/king-papers/documents/man-who-was-fool-sermon-delivered-detroit-council-churches-noon-lenten.

"Martin Luther King Jr.—Nobel Lecture." December 11, 1964. NobelPrize.org. https://www.nobelprize.org/prizes/peace/1964/king/lecture/.

"MIA Mass Meeting at Holt Street Baptist Church." Speech on December 5, 1955, The Martin Luther King, Jr. Research and Education Institute, Stanford University. https://kinginstitute.stanford.edu/king-papers/documents/mia-mass-meeting-holt-street-baptist-church.

"'The Most Durable Power,' Excerpt from Sermon at Dexter Avenue Baptist Church on 6 November 1956." The Martin Luther King, Jr. Research and Education Institute, Stanford

University. https://kinginstitute.stanford.edu/king-papers/documents/most-durable
-power-excerpt-sermon-dexter-avenue-baptist-church-6-november-1956.

"Non-Aggression Procedures to Interracial Harmony." Address Delivered at the
American Baptist Assembly and American Home Mission Agencies Conference,
July 23, 1956, The Martin Luther King, Jr. Research and Education Institute, Stanford
University. https://kinginstitute.stanford.edu/king-papers/documents
/non-aggression-procedures-interracial-harmony-address-delivered-american.

"The Other America." Speech at Stanford University, 1967, The Martin Luther King, Jr.
Center for Nonviolent Social Change, Video, July 2, 2015. https://www.youtube.com
/watch?v=dOWDtDUKz-U.

"Pilgrimage to Nonviolence." April 13, 1960, The Martin Luther King, Jr. Research and
Education Institute, Stanford University. https://kinginstitute.stanford.edu/king
-papers/documents/pilgrimage-nonviolence.

"The Purpose of Education." January 1, 1947, to February 28, 1947, The Martin Luther King,
Jr. Research and Education Institute, Stanford University. https://kinginstitute
.stanford.edu/king-papers/documents/purpose-education.

"Sermon at Temple Israel of Hollywood." February 26, 1965, American Rhetoric. https://
www.americanrhetoric.com/speeches/mlktempleisraelhollywood.htm.

"Speech at the Great March on Detroit." June 23, 1963, University of Virginia. http://
xroads.virginia.edu/~public/civilrights/a0121.html.

"Statement on Ending the Bus Boycott." December 20, 1956, The Martin Luther King, Jr.
Research and Education Institute, Stanford University. https://kinginstitute
.stanford.edu/king-papers/documents/statement-ending-bus-boycott.

"Transcript of Dr. Martin Luther King's speech at SMU on March 17, 1966." Southern
Methodist University, January 10, 2014. https://www.smu.edu/News/2014/mlk-at
-smu-transcript-17march1966.

"What's Your Life's Blueprint?" Speech at Barratt Junior High School in Philadelphia,
October 26, 1967, The Seattle Times. https://projects.seattletimes.com/mlk/words
-blueprint.html#:~:text=Six-months-before-he-was,What-is-your-life's-blueprint%3F.

"Where Do We Go from Here?" Speech in Atlanta, Georgia, on August 16, 1967, The
Martin Luther King, Jr. Research and Education Institute, Stanford University.
https://kinginstitute.stanford.edu/where-do-we-go-here.

"Youth March for Integrated Schools." April 18, 1959, The Martin Luther King, Jr. Research
and Education Institute, Stanford University. https://kinginstitute.stanford.edu
/king-papers/documents/address-youth-march-integrated-schools-18-april-1959.

Books

Bridges, Ruby. *Ruby Bridges Goes to School: My True Story*. New York: Scholastic, Inc., 2003.

Cline-Ransome, Lesa. *She Persisted: Claudette Colvin*. New York: Penguin/Philomel Books, 2021.

Crawford, Vicki L., Jacqueline Anne Rouse, and Barbara Woods, eds. *Women in the Civil Rights Movement: Trailblazers & Torchbearers 1941–1965*. Bloomington: Indiana University Press, 1990.

Levine, Ellen. *Freedom's Children: Young Civil Rights Tell Their Own Stories*. New York: Puffin Books, 1993.

McKissack, Patricia and Frederick McKissack. *The Civil Rights Movement in America from 1865 to the Present,* second ed. Chicago: Children's Press, 1991.

Millender, Dharathula H. *Martin Luther King, Jr. Young Man with a Dream*. New York: Aladdin Paperbacks/Simon & Schuster, 1983.

Rhuday-Perkovich, Olugbemisola. *The Civil Rights Movement (A Step into History)*. New York: Scholastic, Inc., 2018.

Rochelle, Belinda. *Witnesses to Freedom: Young People Who Fought for Civil Rights*. New York, Puffin Books, 1993.

Schwartz, Heather E. *Freedom Riders: A Primary Source Exploration of the Struggle for Racial Justice*. New York: Capstone Press, 2014.

Tisby, Jemar, with Josh Mosey. *How to Fight Racism: A Guide to Standing Up for Racial Justice, Young Reader's Edition*. Grand Rapids: Zonderkidz, 2022.

Washington, James Melvin, ed. *I Have a Dream: Writings and Speeches that Changed the World*. New York: HarperOne, 1986.

Wilkerson, Isabel. *Caste: The Origins of Our Discontents*. New York: Random House, 2020.

Online Sources

"1. Demographic trends and economic well-being." *On Views of Race and Inequality, Blacks and Whites Are Worlds Apart*, Pew Research Center, June 27, 2016. https://www.pewresearch.org/social-trends/2016/06/27/1-demographic-trends-and-economic-well-being/.

"10 Artworks that Defined the Civil Rights Era." *Artsper Magazine*, February 15, 2022. https://blog.artsper.com/en/a-closer-look/10-artworks-that-defined-the-civil-rights-era.

"16th Street Baptist Church Bombing (1963)." National Park Service, https://www.nps.gov /articles/16thstreetbaptist.htm.

"The 1963 March on Washington: A Quarter Million People and a Dream." NAACP. https://naacp.org/find-resources/history-explained/1963-march-washington.

Britannica, The Editors of Encyclopedia. "Poor People's Campaign." *Encyclopedia Britannica*, June 12, 2022. https://www.britannica.com/topic/Poor-Peoples-March.

"Building the Memorial." Martin Luther King, Jr. Memorial. National Park Service. https:// www.nps.gov/mlkm/learn/building-the-memorial.htm.

Callahan, Nancy. "Freedom Quilting Bee." *Encyclopedia of Alabama*, August 8, 2008. https://encyclopediaofalabama.org/article/freedom-quilting-bee/.

"Children's Crusade of 1963: American Freedom Stories (Biography)." History Channel, Video, January 10, 2014. https://www.youtube.com/watch?v=WV0k-3Hkjsw.

Cohen, Sascha. "Why the Woolworth's Sit-In Worked." *Time*, February 2, 2015. https:// time.com/3691383/woolworths-sit-in-history/.

"C-SPAN Cities Tour - Raleigh: 'Freedom's Teacher: The Life of Septima Clark.'" *C-SPAN*, June 14, 2013. YouTube video 8:55, https://www.youtube.com/watch?v=mQpZeAvV-84.

Dear, John. "The God at Dr. King's kitchen table." *National Catholic Reporter*, January 16, 2007. https://www.ncronline.org/blogs/road-peace/god-dr-kings-kitchen-table.

DeSilver, Drew. "Who's poor in America? 50 years into the 'War on Poverty,' a data portrait." Pew Research Center, January 13, 2014. https://www.pewresearch.org /fact-tank/2014/01/13/whos-poor-in-america-50-years-into-the-war-on-poverty -a-data-portrait/.

"Dr. Martin Luther King, Jr. speaks at Christ Church Cathedral in St. Louis." *St. Louis Post-Dispatch*, March 23, 1964. https://www.newspapers.com/clip/39318387/dr-martin -luther-king-jr-speaks-at/?fbclid=IwAR0FEOzh0znKV10s- 0oVD0iXVBsXmkDIUviiRAMg5NKUe44h-YVD9FFtBQI.

Fox, Margalit. "Izola Ware Curry, Who Stabbed King in 1958, Dies at 98." *The New York Times*, March 22, 2015. https://www.nytimes.com/2015/03/22/us/izola-ware-curry -who-stabbed-king-in-1958-dies-at-98.html.

Francis, Roy. " 'Tell them about the dream Martin'-remembering Mahalia Jackson." *Christian Today*, January 27, 2022. https://www.christiantoday.com/article/tell.them .about.the.dream.martin.remembering.mahalia.jackson/138072.htm.

Furman, Daniella. "Freedom Summer, 56 Years Later." National Archives, June 18, 2020. https://rediscovering-black-history.blogs.archives.gov/2020/06/18/freedom -summer-1964/.

Hampton, Alexis. "In 1964, a white, off-duty policeman killed a Black teenager in New York. That led to the now-infamous Harlem race riots." *Insider*, January 29, 2023. https://www.insider.com/harlem-race-riots-1964-history-police-brutality-new-york-2023-1.

Hartlaub, Peter. "Martin Luther King Jr.'s '67 speech left mark on UC Berkeley." SFGATE, May 13, 2014. https://www.sfgate.com/bayarea/article/Martin-Luther-King-Jr-s-67-speech-left-mark-on-5475925.php.

History.com Editors. "Watts Rebellion." History.com, June 24, 2020. https://www.history.com/topics/1960s/watts-riots.

"Is the KKK a Christian Organization?" *Got Questions*. https://www.gotquestions.org/KKK-Christian.html.

"King, Coretta Scott." *The Martin Luther King, Jr. Encyclopedia*, The Martin Luther King, Jr. Research and Education Institute, Stanford University. https://kinginstitute.stanford.edu/encyclopedia/king-coretta-scott.

"The King Philosophy—Nonviolence 365©: The King Center's Definition of Nonviolence." The King Center. https://thekingcenter.org/about-tkc/the-king-philosophy/.

Kratz, Jessie. "LBJ and MLK." *Pieces of History*, National Archives, February 28, 2018. https://prologue.blogs.archives.gov/2018/02/28/lbj-and-mlk/.

Lanese, Jim. "The Desegregation of Cleveland Public Schools: A 40-Year Struggle for Public School Equity." Cleveland Historical. https://clevelandhistorical.org/items/show/813.

Lewis, John. "Opinion: Forgiving George Wallace." *The New York Times*, September 16, 1998. https://www.nytimes.com/1998/09/16/opinion/forgiving-george-wallace.html.

Little, Becky. "How Martin Luther King Jr. Took Inspiration From Gandhi on Nonviolence." *Biography*, January 19, 2021. https://www.biography.com/activists/martin-luther-king-jr-gandhi-nonviolence-inspiration.

Menand, Louis. "When Martin Luther King, Jr., Became a Leader." *The New Yorker*, April 4, 2018. https://www.newyorker.com/news/daily-comment/when-martin-luther-king-jr-became-a-leader.

"Michelle Obama." National Portrait Gallery, Smithsonian Institute. https://npg.si.edu/learn/classroom-resource/michelle-obama.

Mikulich, Alex. "A last will and testament for freedom." *National Catholic Reporter*, July 19, 2014. https://www.ncronline.org/news/people/last-will-and-testament-freedom.

National Park Service. "Out of the Mountain of Despair, a Stone of Hope." https://www
.nps.gov/mlkm/index.htm.

"National Poverty in America Awareness Month: January 2023." United States Census
Bureau, January 2023. https://www.census.gov/newsroom/stories/poverty
-awareness-month.html.

Paulsen, David. "Episcopal martyr Jonathan Myrick Daniels honored in online
commemorations." *Episcopal News Service*, August 17, 2020. https://www
.episcopalnewsservice.org/2020/08/17/episcopal-martyr-jonathan-myrick-daniels
-honored-in-online-commemorations/.

"Rev. Bruce Klunder." Southern Poverty Law Center, April 7, 1964, Southern Poverty Law
Center. https://www.splcenter.org/rev-bruce-klunder.

"SCLC History." Southern Christian Leadership Conference. https://nationalsclc.org
/about/history/.

"Septima Clark." South Carolina ETV. Video, November 14, 2014. https://youtu.be/
yd5kP1fGdDE.

"Shuttlesworth, Fred Lee." *The Martin Luther King, Jr. Encyclopedia*, The Martin
Luther King, Jr. Research and Education Institute, Stanford University. https://
kinginstitute.stanford.edu/encyclopedia/shuttlesworth-fred-lee.

Staff of The Klan Watch Project. "Ku Klux Klan: A History of Racism and Violence." The
Southern Poverty Law Center, sixth edition, 2011. https://www.splcenter.org/sites
/default/files/Ku-Klux-Klan-A-History-of-Racism.pdf.

Stevens, Kyes, "Gee's Bend." *Encyclopedia of Alabama*, March 9, 2007. http://
encyclopediaofalabama.org/article/h-1094.

"Songs and the Civil Rights Movement." *The Martin Luther King, Jr. Encyclopedia,* The
Martin Luther King, Jr., Research and Education Institute, Stanford University.
https://kinginstitute.stanford.edu/encyclopedia/songs-and-civil-rights-movement.

"Southern Christian Leadership Conference (SCLC)." National Park Service. https://www
.nps.gov/subjects/civilrights/sclc.htm.

"The Story Of King's 'Beyond Vietnam' Speech." National Public Radio, March 30, 2010.
https://www.npr.org/2010/03/30/125355148/the-story-of-kings-beyond-vietnam
-speech.

Tate, Allison Slater. "When a mom takes a stand . . . meet Ieshia Evans, mother and nurse
in iconic photo." *TODAY*, July 12, 2016. https://www.today.com/parents/photo
-mother-protesting-baton-rouge-caught-world-s-attention-t100729.

"Thurgood Marshall: LDF Founder and President and Director-Counsel, 1940–1961."
Legal Defense Fund. https://www.naacpldf.org/about-us/history/thurgood
-marshall/.

Tomlin, C.M. "African American Heroes: Thurgood Marshall." *National Geographic Kids*.
https://kids.nationalgeographic.com/history/article/thurgood-marshall.

"Watts Riots." Civil Rights Digital Library. https://crdl.usg.edu/events/watts_riots/.

"Woman in Baton Rouge protest photo: 'Silence speaks volumes.'" CBS, July 15, 2016.
https://www.cbsnews.com/news/ieshia-evans-woman-iconic-baton-rouge-police
-protests-photo-speaks-out/.

Additional Sources for Activist Profiles

Audrey Faye Hendricks

Levinson, Cynthia. *The Youngest Marcher: The Story of Audrey Faye Hendricks, a Young
Civil Rights Activist*. New York: Athenium Books, 2017.

National Civil Rights Museum, "The Children Shall Lead Them: Birmingham 1963." https://
www.civilrightsmuseum.org/news/posts/childrens-c.

PBS LearningMedia. "Audrey Hendricks." Video. https://www.pbslearningmedia.org
/resource/iml04.soc.ush.civil.ahendric/audrey-hendricks/.

Rothberg, Emma. "Audrey Faye Hendricks." National Women's History Museum.
https://www.womenshistory.org/education-resources/biographies/audrey-faye
-hendricks.

Ruby Bridges

Bridges, Ruby. *Ruby Bridges Goes to School: My True Story*. New York: Scholastic, Inc.,
2003.

Scholastic. "Celebrating Ruby Bridges," Video, October 12, 2021. https://www.youtube
.com/watch?v=dkMDD2L70Sg.

Scholastic. "Ruby Bridges Remembers." Video, October 12, 2021. https://youtu.be
/5CgTYGI2mi8.

Sheyann Webb

Daniels, Eugene. "She witnessed Bloody Sunday in person. 58 years later, she'll go back
again." *Politico*, March 4, 2023. https://www.politico.com/news/2023/03/04/bloody
-sunday-witness-58-years-later-00085480.

Lawson, Valerie. "2 women who marched on Bloody Sunday remember John Lewis."
WSFA12 News, July 21, 2020. https://www.wsfa.com/2020/07/21/women-who
-marched-bloody-sunday-remember-john-lewis/.

McGee, Lilly. "The Women of Bloody Sunday." League of Women Voters, March 4, 2022.
https://www.lwv.org/blog/women-bloody-sunday.

"Meet the Hero: Sheyann Webb." Lowell Milken Center for Unsung Heroes. https://
www.lowellmilkencenter.org/programs/projects/view/pigtails-and-protests/hero.

Nolan Donovan, Maggie. "Sheyann Webb: A Story for First Grade." Civil Rights Teaching.
https://www.civilrightsteaching.org/voting-rights/sheyann-webb.

"Sheyann Webb-Christburg: Civil Rights Activist and Author of *Selma, Lord, Selma*."
Eagles Talent Speakers Bureau. https://www.eaglestalent.com/sheyann-webb
-christburg/.

"Sheyann Webb-Christburg." *BK2BAMA*. https://bec2bama.org/instructor/sheyann
-webb-christburg/.

Robert Avery

Matthews, David and James Polk. "5 faces of the March on Washington." CNN,
August 25, 2013. https://www.cnn.com/2013/08/23/us/march-on-washington
-vignettes/index.html.

Norris, Michele. "Determined To Reach 1963 March, Teen Used Thumb And Feet."
National Public Radio, August 14, 2013. https://www.npr.org/2013/08/14/210470828
/determined-to-reach-1963-march-teen-used-thumb-and-feet.

John Lewis

"African American Heritage: Selma Marches." National Archives. https://www.archives.
gov/research/african-americans/vote/selma-marches.

"John Lewis." National Park Service, September 4, 2013. https://www.nps.gov/subjects
/civilrights/john-lewis.htm.

Labode, Modupe. "John Lewis and Good Trouble." National Museum of American
History, July 18, 2020. https://americanhistory.si.edu/blog/john-lewis.

Lewis, John. *Across That Bridge: A Vision for Change and the Future of America*.
Legacy Lit, 2017.

Tamburin, Adam. "'An American story': Nashville street where John Lewis led sit-ins now
bears his name." *The Tennessean,* July 15, 2021. https://www.tennessean.com/story
/news/local/2021/07/15/nashville-honors-john-lewis-weekend-celebration/7927340002/.

Waggoner, Cassandra. "John Lewis (1949–2020)." BlackPast.org, February 19, 2008. https://www.blackpast.org/african-american-history/lewis-john-r-1940/.

Charles Bonner

"Charles Bonner." SNCC Legacy Project. https://snccdigital.org/people/charles-bonner/.

"Oral History/Interview: Charles Bonner and Bettie Mae Fikes." Civil Rights Movement Archive, 2005. https://www.crmvet.org/nars/chuckbet.htm.

Marilyn Luper

"Marilyn Luper Hildreth oral history interview conducted by Joseph Mosnier in Oklahoma City, Oklahoma, 2011 May 24." Library of Congress. https://www.loc.gov/item /2015669111/.

"Marilyn Luper: Daughter of Civil Rights Activist Clara Luper." Interview by John Erling. Voices of Oklahoma, April 7, 2016. https://www.voicesofoklahoma.com/interviews /luper-marilyn.

Ernest Green

Blackside, Inc. "Interview with Ernest Green." University Libraries (Washington University in St. Louis). Video. http://repository.wustl.edu/concern/videos/4b29b798t.

Bunch, Lonnie. "The Little Rock Nine." The National Museum of African American History and Culture/Smithsonian. https://nmaahc.si.edu/explore/stories/little-rock-nine.

"Ernest Green." *The History Makers*, January 22, 2003. https://www.thehistorymakers.org /biography/ernest-green-39.

Glinn, Burt. "On This Day in History: The Little Rock Nine Start School." *Magnum Photos*. https://www.magnumphotos.com/newsroom/society/on-this-day-in-history-the -little-rock-nine-start-school/.

Jaynes, Gerald D. "Little Rock Nine." *Encyclopedia Britannica*. https://www.britannica .com/topic/Little-Rock-Nine.

Claudette Colvin

Adler, Margot. "Before Rosa Parks, There Was Claudette Colvin." National Public Radio, March 15, 2009. https://www.npr.org/2009/03/15/101719889/before-rosa-parks -there-was-claudette-colvin.

Cline-Ransome, Lesa. *She Persisted: Claudette Colvin*. New York: Penguin/Philomel Books, 2021.

Diane Nash

Cheng, Lucia. "Meet Diane Nash, the Civil Rights Icon Awarded the U.S. Highest Civilian Honor." *Smithsonian Magazine*, July 7, 2022. https://www.smithsonianmag.com /smart-news/diane-nash-presidential-medal-freedom-civil-rights-180980380/.

Sources for Quotations of Dr. Martin Luther King Jr.

1. "Darkness cannot drive out darkness, only light can do that. Hate cannot drive out hate, only love can do that."

   Strength to Love

2. "You are as good as anyone."

   Stride Toward Freedom

3. "They came to see that it was ultimately more honorable to walk the streets in dignity than to ride the buses in humiliation."

   "Pilgrimage to Nonviolence"

4. "We were inspired with a desire to give to our young a true sense of their own stake in freedom and justice. We believed they would have the courage to respond to our call."

   Why We Can't Wait

5. "I still have a dream . . . that one day this nation will rise up and live out the true meaning of its creed—'we hold these truths to be self-evident; that all men are created equal'."

   "An Experiment of Love," *A Testament of Hope: The Essential Writings and Speeches of Martin Luther King Jr.*

6. "Human worth lies in relatedness to God. An individual has value because he has value to God. Whenever this is recognized, 'whiteness' and 'blackness' pass away . . . and 'son' and 'brother' are substituted."

   "The Ethical Demands for Integration," *A Testament of Hope: The Essential Writings and Speeches of Martin Luther King Jr.*

7. "Our fears assume many different disguises and dress themselves in strangely different robes."

> "The Mastery of Fear or Antidotes for Fear," *The Papers of Martin Luther King, Jr. Volume VI: Advocate of the Social Gospel, September 1948–March 1963*

8. "*Unity* has never meant *uniformity*."

> *Why We Can't Wait*

9. "The aftermath of nonviolence is the creation of the beloved community, while the aftermath of violence is tragic bitterness."

> "The Power of Nonviolence." *A Testament of Hope: The Essential Writings and Speeches of Martin Luther King Jr.*

10. "Injustice anywhere is a threat to justice everywhere. We are caught in an inescapable network of mutuality, tied in a single garment of destiny. Whatever affects one directly, affects all indirectly."

> "Letter from Birmingham Jail"

11. "We must learn to live together as brothers or perish together as fools."

> "The Man Who Was a Fool," Sermon Delivered at the Detroit Council of Churches' Noon Lenten Services

12. "Let us remember that there is a creative force in this universe working to pull down the gigantic mountains of evil, a power that is able to make a way out of no way and transform dark yesterdays into bright tomorrows."

> "Where Do We Go From Here?"

13. "You young people . . . have somehow discovered the central fact of American life—that the extension of democracy for all Americans depends upon complete integration of Negro Americans."

> "Speech before the Youth March for Integrated Schools"

14. "We shall overcome because the arc of the moral universe is long but it bends toward justice."

> "If The Negro Wins, Labor Wins," *A Testament of Hope: The Essential Writings and Speeches of Martin Luther King, Jr.*

15. "Their death says to us that we must work passionately and unrelentingly for the realization of the American dream."

"Eulogy for the Young Victims of the 16th Street Baptist Church Bombing"

16. "Let no man pull you so low as to hate him."

"The Most Durable Power"

17. "I believe that unarmed truth and unconditional love will have the final word in reality. This is why right, temporarily defeated, is stronger than evil triumphant."

"Acceptance Speech"

18. "When it is dark enough you can see the stars."

Strength to Love

19. "Go back to Mississippi; go back to Alabama; go back to South Carolina; go back to Georgia; go back to Louisiana; go back to the slums and ghettos of the northern cities, knowing that somehow this situation can and will be changed. Let us not wallow in the valley of despair."

"I Have A Dream," *A Testament of Hope: The Essential Writings and Speeches of Martin Luther King, Jr.*

20. "I believe that even amid today's mortar bursts and whining bullets, there is still hope for a brighter tomorrow."

"Acceptance Speech"

21. "A riot is the language of the unheard."

"The Other America"

22. "With this faith we will be able to hew out of the mountain of despair a stone of hope."

"I Have A Dream," *A Testament of Hope: The Essential Writings and Speeches of Martin Luther King Jr.*

23. "Love is the only force capable of transforming an enemy into a friend."

Strength to Love

24. "I have decided to love. . . . If you are seeking the highest good, I think you can find it through love."

"Where Do We Go From Here?"

25. "Let us not seek to satisfy our thirst for freedom by drinking from the cup of bitterness and hatred."

"I Have A Dream," A Testament of Hope: The Essential
Writings and Speeches of Martin Luther King Jr.

26. "He who works against community is working against the whole of creation. . . . I can only close the gap in broken community by meeting hate with love."

Stride Toward Freedom: The Montgomery Story

27. "Forgiveness is not an occasional act; it is a permanent attitude."

Strength to Love

28. "Nonviolence seeks not to humiliate and not to defeat the oppressor, but it seeks to win his friendship and his understanding."

"Non-Aggression Procedures to Interracial Harmony"

29. "I have the audacity to believe that peoples everywhere can have three meals a day for their bodies, education and culture for their minds, and dignity, equality and freedom for their spirits."

"Acceptance Speech"

30. "Oppressed people cannot remain oppressed forever."

"Letter from Birmingham Jail"

31. "The first question which the priest and the Levite asked was: 'If I stop to help this man, what will happen to me?' But . . . the good Samaritan reversed the question: 'If I do not stop to help this man, what will happen to him?'"

Strength to Love

32. "The true neighbor is the man who will risk his position, his prestige and even his life for the welfare of others."

"On Being a Good Neighbor"

33. "In the end, we will remember not the words of our enemies, but the silence of our friends."

A Testament of Hope: The Essential Writings and
Speeches of Martin Luther King Jr.

34. "As a result of their disciplined, nonviolent, yet courageous struggle, they have been able to do wonders in the South, and in our nation."

"The Drum Major Instinct," *A Testament of Hope: The Essential*
Writings and Speeches of Martin Luther King Jr.

35. "It seemed as though I could hear the quiet assurance of an inner voice, saying, 'Stand up for righteousness, stand up for truth. God will be at your side forever.'"

Strength to Love

36. "True nonviolent resistance is not unrealistic submission to evil power. It is rather a courageous confrontation of evil by the power of love."

"My Trip to the Land of Gandhi," *A Testament of Hope: The*
Essential Writings and Speeches of Martin Luther King Jr.

37. "Nonviolent resistance is not a method for cowards."

"An Experiment in Love," *A Testament of Hope: The Essential*
Writings and Speeches of Martin Luther King Jr.

38. "Courage is an inner resolution to go forward in spite of obstacles and frightening situations."

Strength to Love

39. "The ultimate measure of a man is not where he stands in moments of comfort and convenience, but where he stands at times of challenge and controversy."

Strength to Love

40. "It is not enough to say 'We must not wage war.' It is necessary to love peace and sacrifice for it."

"Martin Luther King Jr. Nobel Lecture"

41. "We are determined here in Montgomery to work and fight until justice runs down like water, and righteousness like a mighty stream."

"MIA Mass Meeting at Holt Street Baptist Church"

42. "Give us the ballot, and we will no longer have to worry the federal government about our basic rights."

"Give Us the Ballot"

43. "I have a dream that my four little children will one day live in a nation where they will not be judged by the color of their skin, but by the content of their character."

"I Have A Dream," A Testament of Hope: The Essential Writings and Speeches of Martin Luther King Jr.

44. "Free at last! Free at last! Thank God Almighty, we are free at last!"

"I Have A Dream," A Testament of Hope: The Essential Writings and Speeches of Martin Luther King Jr.

45. "True peace is not merely the absence of tension; it is the presence of justice."

Stride Toward Freedom

46. "It all boils down to the fact that we must never allow ourselves to become satisfied with unattained goals."

"Sermon at Temple Israel of Hollywood"

47. "And there is, deep down within all of us, an instinct. It's a kind of drum major instinct—a desire to be out front, a desire to lead the parade, a desire to be first."

"The Drum Major Instinct," A Testament of Hope: The Essential Writings and Speeches of Martin Luther King Jr.

48. "Keep Martin Luther King in the background and God in the foreground and everything will be all right. Remember you are a channel of the gospel and not the source."

The Autobiography of Martin Luther King, Jr.

49. "Intelligence plus character—that is the goal of true education."

"The Purpose of Education"

50. "Be a bush if you can't be a tree. If you can't be a highway, just be a trail. If you can't be a sun, be a star. For it isn't by size that you win or fail. Be the best of whatever you are."

"What's Your Life's Blueprint?"

51. "Time is neutral; it can be used constructively or destructively."

"Love, Law, and Civil Disobedience," *A Testament of Hope: The Essential Writings and Speeches of Martin Luther King Jr.*

52. "Nonviolence is a powerful and just weapon. Indeed, it is a weapon unique in history, which cuts without wounding and ennobles the man who wields it."

"Martin Luther King Jr. Nobel Lecture"

53. "We want all of our rights, we want them here, and we want them now."

"Speech at the Great March on Detroit"

54. "Make a career of humanity. Commit yourself to the noble struggle for equal rights. You will make a better person of yourself, a greater nation of your country, and a finer world to live in."

"Speech before the Youth March for Integrated Schools"

55. "The means we use must be as pure as the ends we seek."

"Letter from Birmingham Jail"

56. "Let freedom ring."

"I Have A Dream," *A Testament of Hope: The Essential Writings and Speeches of Martin Luther King Jr.*

57. "For when people get caught up with that which is right and they are willing to sacrifice for it, there is no stopping point short of victory."

"I've Been to the Mountaintop"

58. "If a man hasn't discovered something that he will die for, he isn't fit to live."

"Speech at SMU on March 17, 1966"

59. "I just want to do God's will."

"I've Been to the Mountaintop"

60. "The struggle to eliminate the evil of racial injustice constitutes one of the major struggles of our time."

"Martin Luther King Jr. Nobel Lecture"

ABOUT THE CREATORS

DR. MARTIN LUTHER KING JR. (1929–1968), civil rights leader and recipient of the Nobel Prize for Peace, inspired and sustained the struggle for freedom, nonviolence, interracial brotherhood, and equality.

LISA A. CRAYTON is a versatile nonfiction editor and writer with more than thirty years' experience. She writes devotionals, articles, Bible study guides, and nonfiction titles for adults and children. Lisa has an MFA in creative writing, is a coregional advisor for her local SCBWI chapter, and is participating in Alfred Street's "Minister in Training" program.

SHARIFA STEVENS is the daughter of Jamaican immigrants. She has earned a bachelor degree in African American Studies and a master in theology. Sharifa aspires to use writing as a vehicle that moves readers to intersect with the sacred and the honest. Sharifa is married to a Renaissance man and mother to two lively boys. They live in Dallas, TX.

CAMILLA RU is a Zimbabwean-British illustrator and designer. Her work incorporates her African roots as well as her love of vibrant patterns and colors and her passion for connecting people through representation. She enjoys exploring various forms of creativity and welcomes inspirations from life's experiences to tell stories, expand imaginations, and inspire joy. She has had the privilege of working on various projects, from editorial work to literary work, promotional artwork, and more.